Voices of Readers

Voices of Readers

How We Come to Love Books

G. Robert Carlsen

Anne Sherrill

National Council of Teachers of English
1111 Kenyon Road, Urbana, Illinois 61801

NCTE Editorial Board: Donald R. Gallo, Thomas Newkirk, Raymond J. Rodrigues, Dorothy S. Strickland, Brooke Workman, L. Jane Christensen, *ex officio*, John Lansingh Bennett, *ex officio*

Staff Editor: Robert A. Heister

Cover Design: Michael J. Getz

Interior Book Design: Tom Kovacs for TGK Design

NCTE Stock Number 56398

Library of Congress Cataloging-in-Publication Data

Carlsen, G. Robert, 1917–
    Voices of readers : how we come to love books / G. Robert Carlsen, Anne Sherrill.
        p.   cm.
    ISBN 0–8141–5639–8
    1. Books and reading — United States.   2. Children — United States — Books and reading.   3. Librarians — United States — Books and reading.   4. Teachers — United States — Books and reading.
I. Sherrill, Anne.   II. Title.
Z1003.2.C37   1988
028'.9 — dc19   87-37541

Contents

Subject (600, 610, 650)	
Geographic (651)	
Genre/form (655)	
Added author (700, 710)	

Possible other notes[1]: organization and arrangement (351); citation (510); additional physical forms (digital, mirographic, etc.) (530); reproduction (533); location of originals (535); terms of reproduction (540); associated materials (544); language (546); publication (581); conservation

Acknowledgments

We are grateful to the thousands of students who passed through our classes and who wrote the original autobiographies from which the protocols in this book have been extracted. We especially mention Dr. Dale Paul Hauser, whose complete paper begins chapter 1. Dr. Hauser, then a student at the University of Iowa, is at present an English instructor at Kirkwood Community College in Cedar Rapids, Iowa.

Mary and Ambrose Manning, professors emeriti from East Tennessee State University, helped enormously with their reading and editing of the final manuscript as did William Irmscher, professor emeritus from the University of Washington in Seattle.

Special mention goes to Ruth Christoffer Carlsen, who learned to use a computer so she could type and edit the manuscript from its inception through to the finished product. In the process, she probably read the manuscript more times and more thoroughly than anyone else.

Introduction

How does a person come to acquire a love for literature? Does one's love of literature come about because of an inherited trait, or because of environmental conditioning? Is it due to the kind of person one is, or is it brought about by the culture in which one grows up? When I began teaching college students, I could speculate only in terms of my own experience. My parents were both college graduates. They did read an occasional book, but their principal reading fare consisted of magazines, newspapers, and legal briefs. Each of the houses we lived in had a built-in bookcase about waist high on either side of the fireplace. These bookcases were adequate to contain a few gift books, some old college texts, *The Book of Knowledge*, the Bible, a dictionary, and an occasional contemporary novel.

What, then, lured me toward reading and literature? Why did I become a reader while my two brothers, one older and one younger, did not (at least until fairly late in their lives) find the magic in books? I was always the "different one" in our family — the odd man out so to speak — so I assumed that my experiences with literature while growing up just represented some peculiarity in me. Therefore, I kept my experiences pretty much to myself. It never occurred to me to talk about this "idiosyncrasy" with anybody else. In college, I majored in English, not so much by design as by taking courses I liked.

Eventually, my career led me to training secondary school English teachers and trying to help them make literature meaningful for the young people in their classes. One summer I was invited to teach English teachers in Hawaii. They were a mixture of native Hawaiians, first generation Chinese, Japanese, Koreans, and Portuguese as well as a handful of West Coast teachers — about 60 students in all. Up to this point, I had spent my life largely around midwesterners, so this group in Hawaii seemed exotic, remote, and unique. Many had grown up on the pineapple and sugar plantations of the islands. Most had never known the confining quality of winter or the snug comfort of reading in front of a fireplace.

To better understand their experience with books and reading, I asked them to write what I called a "reading autobiography." In doing so, they needed to reflect upon a number of questions. (What did they remember about learning to read? What books did they remember reading? Who, if anyone, had been important in developing their attitudes toward reading? When and where did they read?) What a surprise I had when I read the sixty papers. Although they came from very different backgrounds, both culturally and environmentally, the members of the group described experiences with books while growing up that were almost identical to my own in Minneapolis. After all, my experience was not unique. So from that time on, the reading autobiography became a regular part of my assignments in "Literature for Adolescents." My collection now numbers in the thousands and spans the years from the mid-1950s to the mid-1980s. These voices from all parts of the country speak about their experiences with reading.

I discovered that, given the chance, adults like to talk about their reading. In order to put this experience into words, one must force the mind to recollect forgotten but important memories of how one became a reader. Most people enjoy the process of exploring these memories. And most, like me, are astounded to see that their experience is not unique at all, but very common.

In the process of discussing the autobiographies in class, the memories of one person would stir kindred memories in another. "Oh," they would say, "I had forgotten about the *Big Little* books until you mentioned them — I must have had all of them. I wonder what ever became of them?" (Those books that survived went into antique bookstores and are now collectors' items, with prices rising steadily as their pulp paper slowly disintegrates.)

In general, this book presents the voices of people who are readers, people who were in classes at the University of Iowa, University of Colorado at Boulder, University of Texas at Austin, University of Hawaii, or East Tennessee State University. They were overwhelmingly librarians or English teachers or were in training to become one or the other. Most were oriented toward reading. Only occasionally did a nonreader surface; usually, this person was a technocrat who was getting a library science degree, or a parent taking the course to see what was recommended for a teenage son or daughter, or a nurse fulfilling a pediatric requirement, or someone looking for an easy course. But the information they supplied is valuable as well. However, the majority were people who, as adults, had a committed interest in books and reading.

The voices in these autobiographies tell us of being spellbound by reading, of where they found books to read, of their frustrations and their triumphs, of *covert* reading, of what happened to them in school classrooms and libraries, of life in their families and with their peers. The autobiographies are filled with surprising revelations and touching confessions.

For the most part, the autobiographies appear in unedited form, thereby preserving the voice of each respondent. In general, the people write well — giving lie to the complaint that our college and university young people cannot turn out a decent sentence. Perhaps because they were exploring an avenue of their lives that was basically meaningful to them, the words to express their findings came more easily. They would seem to prove the claim of modern rhetoricians that people generally write well when they are writing about something that counts.

Maybe the love of reading is inborn. It may spring from a kind of inner compulsion that seems to arise spontaneously. Certainly, the lives of many musicians, artists, dancers, sculptors, and athletes indicate that those individuals were irresistibly drawn to their "first love"; nothing in their background can quite account for it. It has been estimated that readers in our population remain a minority group and that their percentage does not change much from one generation to another. If this is so, it is still interesting to see how these people became avid readers in a culture where reading is largely promoted as a utilitarian activity that is necessary for the basic communication processes between people: for example, road signs, advertisements, bills, contracts, income tax, and so on. What, then, draws one particular group of people to reading as a source of recreation and delight? To what extent does the culture prize and promote this special interest? Does society at large provide any rewards for this enthusiasm?

On the other hand, if reading is not really a matter of our own genes, but is something that individuals develop through their experiences, then these autobiographies indicate directions — they tell what activities and experiences helped to make readers of these people and what impediments stood in their way. The voices in this book, therefore, give us hints of how to go about developing and encouraging readers within our educational and societal framework.

Until very recently, at least, we had put considerable effort into exposing people to literature. There had been a strong feeling that the young should come to know a body of literature in common: for example, *Mother Goose,* the Perrault fairy tales, *Robin Hood,* the Greek myths, some patriotic poetry, *Tom Sawyer* and *Little Women;* later we add Shakespeare and Dickens, George Eliot, Hawthorne and Whitman, and so on. This exposure to a common body of literature is one of the unifying forces in our culture that we strive to give them.

Earlier in the twentieth century, literary study was the pivotal center of the elementary school program. For example, when *Heidi* was to be read, every other subject was somehow related to Switzerland: its geography, its art, its music, and so forth. More recently, such emphasis on a work of literature has given way to an emphasis on the "skill" of reading. The books we term "readers," those elementary texts that center on learning "how" to read and not on the kind of literature read, were once confined to the early grades; however, they are now the standard fare, often through the eighth grade. The secondary school English program that was almost exclusively devoted to literary study is now moving toward an emphasis on composition. If we are to once again center on literature, it is important to know what mature adults feel about their experiences with literature as well as what they feel about their reactions to these experiences. Did their lives benefit from these experiences? What do they see as the purpose and was this purpose achieved for them? Should a set body of "classics" be reinstituted or do their reading patterns give suggestions for better kinds of materials?

Throughout the years, as I gathered and saved all of these student reading autobiographies, I was haunted by the need to put the materials together in a meaningful way so that others might be made aware of the ways in which people came to be readers. At times, I extracted some excerpts and used them in speeches, but I was frustrated by the great mass of materials to be examined, the excerpts to be chosen, and then how to collect those excerpts into a meaningful whole. Rather late in my career, Anne Sherrill came to me to work on a doctoral degree, and in time, she became curious about the cardboard cartons labeled "autobiographies," which were stacked in my office. She became excited about the challenge they presented and chose to use them for her doctoral study. She, too, began using the autobiography as an assignment in her own classes, thereby checking the accuracy and relevance of the autobiographies that had been collected as long as a decade or two earlier. She found that most of the recent recollections were very similar to the earlier ones.

The writers seemed to report on discreet incidents in a chronological order, although at no time were there any instructions issued to follow such a pattern. Often, the memories had an emotional overtone ranging from simple nostalgia, to joy identified with certain books, to anger over a particularly traumatic experience. The problem of the dissertation was to winnow out, from all the various kinds of experiences, specific categories of experience, each of which was either instrumental or detrimental to a person's reading development. It was this pattern, then, that made it possible for the two of us to write this book.

This is not a statistical study. The responses were so freewheeling that counting and figuring percentages did not reveal the real impact of the study. One person might mention Nancy Drew by title, but another would say, "I read series books avidly." As a result, we had to generalize instead of count. Once Sherrill and I had the picture, with all of its details and nuances, we considered constructing a questionnaire in which we asked everyone similar questions: for example, "Did you read surreptitiously when you were not supposed to be reading?" We decided that a questionnaire might be interesting, but that the responses could lose their spontaneity. People might be inclined to cheat a bit and try to give us what they thought we wanted. Because of the unstructured nature of the autobiography, the writers told us what was uppermost in their memories about their reading experiences. They do not tell it all, but they tell the things that are probably of greatest importance to each of them. We also considered studying the collection by decades to see if there were significant changes. However, we discovered that, although the book titles that teenagers read for pleasure had changed, the overall experience with books seemed to follow a consistent pattern throughout the thirty years of study.

If you are a reader, you will often feel as if you are meeting yourself in the following pages. "Oh," you will think, "I too wanted to be a veterinarian when I was reading *Black Beauty.*" On the other hand, you will come across things that are interesting but foreign to your own experience. I, myself, never read under the covers (I never liked the fetid smell), but I find it interesting that so many people did. Sherrill and I sometimes wondered whether this actually happened or whether it was a cliche that people came to believe in because it was expressed so often. When we quizzed our classes about this possibility, they insisted that, yes, they did just this and it was a frequent occurrence. Thus, we have come to feel that these records are honest ones: at least as honest as it is possible for memories to be.

The first set of autobiographies was written thirty years ago, so some of these writers' recollections may, in fact, go back more than fifty years and mention such things as dime stores, houses with attics, and washing dishes at the kitchen sink. The recollections have a nostalgic aura that seems almost quaint. You will find references (possibly some are inaccurate) to books and magazines that are now out of print as well as forgotten; publications such as *The Youth's Companion* and *St. Nicholas Magazine*. But Nancy Drew and the Hardy Boys continue to have an enchanted life and are as popular today as they were fifty years ago. On the other hand, Harold Bell Wright and Grace Livingston Hill, once favorite writers of teenagers, have been supplanted by contemporary writers. Thus, the reading autobiographies from today's students may differ from earlier ones in specific books and authors but not in the general pattern of reading experiences.

First, we shall let these writers outline the overall pattern of their reading as they moved from childhood to adulthood. Most people are amazed to find how similar this pattern is from individual to individual. We tend to think of reading as a private undertaking that is unique to each of us. I know, because I once felt that way too. Then we shall examine, in more detail, some of the recurring experiences with their twisting, turning manifestations: what did people say about teachers and librarians; about oral reading and book reports; about the series books and the classics? At the end we come to no set conclusions but rather to a sense of what direction the curriculum should take if, indeed, we are interested in creating a nation of readers.

G. Robert Carlsen

1 Growing with Books

Let us look first at a sample of a complete autobiography written by a former student, Paul Hauser.

I vaguely remember learning how to read "Run, Spot" and what a good feeling it was to go home and tell my mother about it. But I don't remember many of the books of my early school years. My memory has mixed all of those years together so that it is almost impossible to separate them any longer.

I have three sisters and no brothers, so many of the books that I read in the early days were passed on to me by my two older sisters. There was *Heidi, Little Women,* some Nancy Drew books, *Tom Sawyer* (I can still hear his aunt calling him), and *Pippi Longstocking.* Even though she was a girl, I liked her immensely, and I was forever asking the librarian if there were any more books about her available. That librarian was one of the nicest women I have met . . . her name is on the tip of my tongue . . . Mrs. McGrill. A sweet lady. She was a positive influence, I'm sure, on how I felt about books.

When I got old enough for Cub Scouts, I got *Boys' Life* in the mail. That magazine had some incredibly good short stories. I remember two of them distinctly: one was about a boy who found a time machine and discovered how to operate it (I still dream about it occasionally), and the other was about a boy who had a pet worm. The worm was a genius and communicated telepathically with his friend. He always helped the boy win spelling bees and get A's on tests at school. There were no baseball games for me on the days that my magazine came in the mail. I went to my room and read.

As I grew interested and participated in sports (actually it became a way of life for many years), I found out that there were books about sports and sports heroes too. I read everything I could find for a while. As a matter of fact, I'm still a sucker for a good basketball story. Those I still remember that I particularly enjoyed are: *Fighting Five* (I read that one at least six times,) *The Twenty-third Street Crusaders,* and Bill Bradley's *A Sense of Where You Are.* I also read lots of biographies: Lou Gehrig, Babe Ruth, Knute Rockne and Joe DiMaggio. Most of the other titles are lost by now, but the feeling of going to my room on a winter night and opening one of those books is still with me. It was better than candy, popcorn and even Saturday morning cartoons.

There were the animal stories too. I read every book by Jim Kjelgaard (remember *Big Red*?), many of Jack London's and lots of others which I can't name anymore. I'll never forget *Desert Dog*. In fact, I still think about him crawling into a cave and instinctively covering himself with mud when he was injured. That picture is still clear and often drifts back to my consciousness, although I never know what precipitates it.

My group of buddies passed around Felsen's books — *Hot Rod, Street Rod* and all the others. Why do I have so much trouble with titles? The stories are still with me though. And the characters.

Although I detested history class all the way through school, there were some novels about gladiators that I really enjoyed. They were an exception, though, and only now am I starting to be rid of my aversion for history. Now I am expected to know it and have much catching up to do.

All of the books I have mentioned so far, with the exception of Bradley's, I read before high school and outside of class. When I think back to high school, it is hard to remember what I read. Maybe I quit reading so much then, for there were girlfriends, jobs, cars, sports and dances to take up most of my time. I do remember *Lord of the Flies* making a big impression on me, *The Odyssey* making me nervous (the twelfth grade teacher was intimidating), *Silas Marner* being a bore, and Shakespeare being too much to handle at that time. Other than those, I draw a blank. High school years have many diversions. Many teachers still don't realize that.

My first year of college opened my eyes in many ways, and since then I have been an avid reader. Ayn Rand's *The Fountainhead* was somewhat of a bible for me in those angry-young-man days. So was Kerouac. I finally realized that literature could teach me as well as entertain. Those who have taught me since then include Hemingway, Fitzgerald, Faulkner (my all time favorite, I think), Tolkein, Kafka, Vonnegut (terrific), Updike, Twain, Lessing, Shakespeare, Chaucer, Camus, Wolfe, Kesey, Roth, Fielding, Dickens (a special one for me), Defoe, Proust, Joyce, Williams, Flaubert, Musil . . . Hell, the list could go on and on. It is obvious that fiction was and is my favorite genre by far. Give me a good novel and I'll be content.

When I began teaching, I had some Individualized Reading classes. This was during the time of all the pregnant girl books — *My Darling, My Hamburger, Mr. and Mrs. Bojo Jones*, etc. It would be very hard to read another one. I also got in on a lot of the drug books . . . *Go Ask Alice* . . . for example, but the sex books like Judy Blume's hadn't struck yet. Individualized Reading was a good experience for me. I read a minimum of a book a day while I was teaching the course.

Salinger is one of the very best, and I almost forgot him. I also liked Steinbeck, Burgess, e.e. cummings, Emerson, Thoreau and John Dewey.

Now, besides fiction, I have a strong interest in non-fiction prose. Whether the new journalism is alive or dead, it had a big influence on the freedom of style in non-fiction that writers of late are experimenting with. I also like fantasy, some science fiction, good poetry and sooner or later I will get down to seriously dealing with drama.

As interesting as this single record is, like all of the autobiographies, it is limited by being only one individual's experiences. Obviously, no one person could have all the experiences that lead one to becoming a reader.

Following the introductory comments in each chapter of this book is a collection of excerpts, each from a different autobiography, that we refer to in the text as "protocols." These protocols, some reproduced with minor changes in spelling and punctuation, come from many different writers and tell about certain common experiences with reading. Following the individual comments will be a "reprise" that draws together some of the findings drawn from the extracts as well as from the autobiographies not represented here.

What follows in this chapter is a kind of composite autobiography. We begin with the preschool-age child's encounters with reading. (Please note that, in our book, "preschool" refers to that period before entering a structured, school-type environment — the time period when mass daycare, as we know it today, virtually did not exist.) Then, we arbitrarily divide childhood into two periods, breaking roughly at the end of the third and sixth grades. The earlier period is one in which there are many accounts about learning to read, while in the later period the writers are actually doing reading on their own. However, there are some surprising things that happen along the way.

The junior high school and senior high school experiences seem to divide very neatly from one another. Is this division inherent in a child's maturation? Or is it created by the way the school system is set up and by the expectations brought to bear upon the reader? Perhaps we can come to terms with the problem in later chapters when we examine some of the reactions in greater detail.

Finally, we have put together the college and adult experiences. There are fewer after-college records because so many of the writers were still in college themselves. You may discover contradictory statements within a group of quotations. For instance, some writers report being intrigued with the primers. Others found them incredibly dull. We include both viewpoints in order to show the diversity of responses.

Preschool Years

The first books I can remember are those that my mother used to read to me, and that I soon knew well enough to figure out by myself. I can't remember now though what, if anything, the words meant to me then. I do know, however, that in *From Timbucktoo to Kalamazoo,* I could recognize when the train went from Timbucktoo to Kalamazoo, and to Kalamazoo and back it went "clickety clack, clickety clack," all the way down the track. This was because the words all looked the same and it sounded neat when my mother said it.

My father sang to me. He sang "Little Brown Jug," "Blow the Man Down," and "The Daring Young Man on the Flying Trapeze." Rhythm was important in language and the flavor of anticipation was as real as his cigarette smoke.

I was introduced to books at a very early age thanks to my mother. Every evening before bed, my mother would read chapters from books such as *Old Yeller* and *Black Beauty* to my sister and me. I also remember hearing over and over nursery rhymes from *Childcraft* and stories such as *Millions of Cats.* I was always affected emotionally by sad stories and would make up imaginary sequels to such stories. I also remember imagining I could fly on a goose like Nils in *The Wonderful Adventures of Nils.*

I always loved "Hickory Dickory Dock," because my father used to tickle my back when the mouse ran up the clock.

I, too, quickly learned the rhymes well enough to recite along with my mother and knew the stories well enough that I quickly produced the climaxes of the tales before my mother had the chance!

Rocking me to sleep, my mother used to recite over and over the nursery rhymes from my big book of *Mother Goose.* I became so familiar with the illustrations that I could recite the poems from memory.

In 1957, I went to kindergarten every other day. On my free days I would look forward to a before lunch nap with my mommy who would read Donald Duck comic books to me.

I remember enchanting summer afternoons on an Iowa farm in the mid-twenties with a hammock stretched between the trees and I, a child of four, listening to the pleasant voice of my mother reading to me from one of the series of books called *Brother and*

Sister Books. My favorite story was *Peter Rabbit,* and I used to sit on the floor while my mother or father read about Peter's adventures with Flopsy, Mopsy, and Cottontail. I delighted in the adventurous spirit of Peter and used to go along with him when he went to Farmer Brown's carrot patch, and when he was nearly caught, I shuddered and crooked my neck as if someone had me caught by the nape until he was safely back in the rabbit hole with his family.

Somewhat nebulously, I can recall listening to my father recite poetry to me when I was a child of two or three. They were children's poems . . . things like "Little Jack Horner" and gaudier pieces like "On the Road to Mandalay" and "Gunga Din" and "Abou Ben Adhem." As I became more familiar with the words, we made a game out of reciting them together. I remember that the one I enjoyed most was Leigh Hunt's "Jenny."

I was about four and in the hospital for an operation. An aunt had given me several books that were mostly of a pictorial nature. They were on cardboard, each page, and my mother read them to me again and again. I remember thinking as she read them how nice it must be to know what is going on in the pictures that sometimes were not completely self-explanatory.

One of my first memories is that of my mother reading to me. I liked the sound of the words almost more than their meaning. I loved the pictures in the fairy story books, and I think I used to make up my own versions. It came as something of a shock to me, when I learned to read, that the brothers Grimm and Mr. Andersen did not always agree with me. I also remember a huge book of Gilbert and Sullivan which has been around since I was about five. Mother told me the stories of *H.M.S. Pinafore* and *The Mikado* and she sang me some of the songs. I learned "Buttercup" by heart before I was six. The process of inventing my own tales continued in the first grade . . . I much preferred that Dick do something besides "look, look, look" as he stood on his head in the leaves.

My early memories of my own involvement with literature begin with rich, vivid images in reds, oranges, and warm browns viewed from my bed or my father's lap. Decidedly secure, I was safe to myself in fanciful tales.

Words fascinated me. I heard my father using long medical terms. He would have to continually answer the question, "What does that mean?" I found that if I heard a word and then saw the word that I would take a mental photograph and recognize it when I saw it again. I recognized "polymorphonuclear" before I recognized "dog" and "cat." But meaning had little to do with this process. It was more or less a game to sound words just for the pure noise of the words.

Surprisingly, the story of the book wasn't the main criterion I used for picking favorites, but rather it was the format or appearance of the book. One of my most cherished possessions, I remember, was a picture book of kittens in which the reproductions of the birds were large and in color. Still another was *Bambi*.

Being the second youngest child of a family of eight, I recall mother with a group of three or four of us, sitting in a semi-circle around her chair showing us pictures and telling us the story of "Cinderella," "Jack and the Beanstalk," and other of *Grimm's Fairy Tales*. Cinderella has been my "dream girl" all through the years, because, I believe, she was depicted so beautifully by mother's slow sweet voice.

My inward desire to learn to read on my own was inspired by *Cinderella*. My goal was to read, reread, and live that one story.

Having older brothers and sisters who were able to read was always a challenge. I wanted to read their Christmas books, especially.

My earliest memories of reading centered around the vast numbers of dogs and cats and balls such as found in those books published by Golden Books. These were read to me at convenient times (bedtime, naptime, etc.) until I knew the stories so well that I could read them myself, or at least repeat most of the words from memory.

One of my earliest memories is of patiently following my beloved grandmother all through her household chores while clutching the Sunday funnies. At last she would be through and would read them to me — again and again. Then I would "read" them over and over all the rest of the week.

As I look back on my reading past, I find that my earliest recollection is of the controversial comic books. Having an older brother to keep me supplied, I spent much of my time browsing through comics. None of this time was spent reading them. Instead I found I could follow the story just as well by looking at the pictures. Even now I rely on pictures to guide me through magazines.

Before I could read, I remember having a tremendous desire to read for myself. One picture comes to mind of my standing in front of the book case and thinking, "When I get big, I'm going to read a whole book." An echo of the longing I felt chills me when I think of it.

Reprise

It is not surprising to find that the first memories of books are most often of a mother's reading to an infant. Fathers are remembered almost as often, and occasionally an older brother or sister or a grandmother. Only once in a while is a grandfather mentioned. Almost always, the reading situation with a parent is associated with love, comfort, and security. Most of the reading material is what we might expect: *Mother Goose,* the folk stories, the comics and funnies. But still, a few youngsters remembered getting a thrill out of material ordinarily thought to be beyond them: light opera, verses, adult poetry, a medical text.

It is also natural to expect reports about the importance of pictures to reading. As we know, youngsters usually read pictures before reading words. Anthropologists report that glyphs and hieroglyphs were the first attempts by human beings to tell a story. Perhaps the child is, in part, recapitulating this stage of human development. Given a lively imagination, youngsters can make up their own story to fit a sequence of pictures.

Practically all the accounts tell of favorite books that the writers wanted read to them over and over again. This repetition enhances the listener's ability to memorize and is an early process of learning. When children are subsequently able to tell the story just as it is written, they feel a great sense of ego gratification; children feel that they are, in fact, reading. Understandably, parents and siblings usually praise and encourage this skill. Hence, these children experience warm and happy feelings of success in their association with books.

Pleasure in the sounds of language seems a natural enhancement of the preverbal infant's joy in making noises. (Didn't you enjoy the account of the child who delighted in her father's medical terms?) As we shall see a bit later, such children are often disappointed in primers, perhaps because the controlled vocabularies and uninspired rhythmic patterns pale in comparison to the mouth-filling sounds of "Gunga Din" or "polymorphonuclear."

The preschoolers, being conscious of reading and its rewards, want to read for themselves. They want to be able to decipher what those black marks beneath the pictures will reveal. They play at reading and struggle to unlock the secrets of reading. One of our writers became so enthralled with books that she wanted to write them herself. Although not explicit in these autobiographies, some children scribbled lines on paper and, when questioned, could talk about what they had written.

Preschool experiences with books leave indelible memories. One writer remembered the joy of being tickled when "the mouse runs down the clock," another her continuing love of Cinderella, and still another her physical reaction to Peter Rabbit's capture. How then are these pleasant, first experiences with books related to an individual's success in learning to read? The next section presents accounts of both good and bad memories of learning to read during the early school years.

Early Elementary Years

The first book that I remember well is the *Better Homes and Gardens Story Book*. The book contains many stories, poems by Robert Louis Stevenson and others, fables, and some tales of other countries. My mother often read to me from this book, and when I learned to read, I read and re-read it to myself.

The first book that comes to mind was when I was five or six years old. It was a child's book about a kangaroo and I can remember the satisfaction I felt after reading the whole book by myself. I don't recall the name of it, but I can remember reading it over and over again. Before this time I can remember looking over my mother's shoulder as she read stories to my brother and me.

My dad always read books he had enjoyed, so before I could read very well, I had heard *Tom Sawyer, Huckleberry Finn, Gulliver's Travels* and the Hardy Boys. We could always interrupt and ask questions about things we did not understand. I remember *Huckleberry Finn* in the first grade took lots of explanations, but it was fun to hear Dad try to get the dialect, to hear him laugh at the funny scenes, and to try to follow the raft down the big U.S. map.

When I started school and really learned to read for myself, I gobbled up everything in sight that was near my own reading level. I loved books and loved to read and I remember crying my heart out when the teacher would not let me take home my first reader when we completed it.

The first memory I have of coming into contact with reading that gave me real pleasure was my experience with the "Alice" and "Jerry" books. I can recall nothing of their content, but the vivid sense of mystery and excitement of being transported into a new, colorful and adventurous world has always remained with me.

Finally came the day that I would really learn to read at school. How disappointed I was in the primer books that repeated over and over, "I see. I see mother. I see father."

In first grade we marched through the "Dick and Jane" books. I didn't like them very much. Actually, I suppose I was more neutral toward Dick and Jane than anything else. They didn't really seem to be much like my friends at all.

By the time I entered first grade and was first instructed in the art of reading, I found myself bored and not a little angry at the progress. This happened, I am quite sure, to many youngsters whose parents had exposed them to books, letters, words and associations years before. An unpleasant memory of this period is one of the endless books all saying, "Here is Jack. Run, Jack, run." I remember huge block printing indicating that all six year olds are somewhat blind.

My grandmother was a character and if she read to me it was what she was reading for herself: it ranged from *True Story* to current novels. Of course, if it was a novel I only heard portions, never a complete book. My father read me Swedish nursery rhymes and folk tales in his native tongue. My Mom had five bachelor brothers and as I grew older I remember pestering them to read to me. Now I was introduced to the *Police Gazette* stories. My serious uncle read *National Geographic* articles to me; my poultry raising uncle enlightened me about new breeds and diseases of chickens in the *Poultry Journal*. In first grade . . . the books I could read by myself were so dull compared to the ones I had been exposed to by my relatives.

In third grade my mother asked me to read *Little Women* before I saw the movie. I read all of Louisa May Alcott's books after that and also *Kidnapped, Treasure Island,* and Kipling's *Jungle Book.*

During my grade school period, I was interested in *Winnie the Pooh* read to us during class times in second and third grade and not at all intrigued by what we were reading in class.

In the first grade I was bored, so the teacher let me have a library card and I spent many hours in the library attached to my school. I read all the pre-primers. Then the primers. Then the first and second grade books.

Most of my books were given to me by my two older sisters. I was the baby of the family by nine years and nothing was more fun for my sisters than subjecting me to playing school. They would give me books, copy down the words I didn't know, make me study them, and then test me on the words out of context. Consequently, I went through at least two books a week outside of school during my first and second grades. By the time I was in third grade I could take advantage of my sisters. They read *Alice in Wonderland, Treasure Island, The Wizard of Oz,* and *Heidi* to me.

My grandmother introduced me to the library at a very early age. It was a little branch library about two miles from our house and we walked there once a month. I had few books of my own, but grandmother taught me that the library was a treasure house of books I could share so long as I took good care of them and that the librarians were the kindly guardians of this treasure house.

For years I thought the librarian was the very epitome of the career woman.

It is in second grade that I recall a specific story, *Goody Two Shoes.* And it was at this time that I took my first library card from the big library downtown. I can still feel the awe at the big room of children's books that were at my disposal — such wealth! And wonder of wonders, I could check out four that I wanted: it was like being let loose in a candy shop with instructions to help myself to a nickel's worth.

As a third grader, I started to read, in alphabetical order, my way through the elementary section of our library. I recall reaching "F" and deciding that there must be a better way to select interesting books.

I was the first student in my first grade to read a book aloud to the whole class. *Let's Go to the Zoo.* Not only was reading fun, but it gained me recognition and praise.

In second grade we had a chart and for every book we read we could put a tiny "book" of construction paper next to our name. This became a very competitive game. I don't recall any of the books that I read, but I know I zipped through many so I could be right up there. Most of our grade school reading seemed founded on competition and status.

I remember in second grade I was in the best reading group. Then in the beginning of third grade I was placed in the poorest reading group. My pride must have been hurt, as I remember sitting in a chair in the half-circle in front of the room and just mumbling when it came my turn to read.

I recall a second grade teacher who had a special gift for making reading an exciting experience. She placed a library table in the room: the books on the table were new, attractive and I even remember the way they smelled, an indescribably new-book smell, a scent that even today has pleasurable associations for me.

Reprise

It is not surprising that the first books children want to read as they gain rudimentary reading skills are those favorites read to them by family members. Now that they are in school, they have a new way of making a book their own. Instead of having to depend on someone else to call forth the magic of a favorite book, they can do it themselves through their newly acquired reading ability.

It is natural to want to practice a new skill. Many of these respondents recalled "gobbling up" books and treasuring the early school experiences as a continuation of pleasant family associations with reading during those preschool years. Even the standard primers were termed exciting by a few of the respondents. But over and over again, we found that the writers expressed boredom with primers, probably because the primers were dull when compared with the materials read to them at home. Before their meeting with "Dick and Jane," many of the respondents had associated literature with excitement and fascinating word sounds. Now, books gave them innocuous plots full of dull repetition. It is interesting to note that a few writers mentioned the large print of primers as if, for some reason, six-year-olds have need of large print.

Primers receive few words of outright praise, yet their proclaimed "dullness" did not seem to stifle the overall reading interest of the youngsters. The early school years find children seeking out books regardless of what they consider the quality of their school reading. The children find books on grandmother's bookshelves, in their siblings' rooms, in friends' supplies, and it is in these early years that most seem to discover the library. A first library card opens up a fascinating, new mother lode of books and usually marks the onset of a lifelong reading habit.

The early school years also offer some special and varied reading experiences. Some young people find reading as one way of gaining status. Others take pride in being permitted to read aloud to the class. Contests help to snag many fledgling readers; prizes for reading quantities of books are sometimes offered during these years and the process accelerates later on. In the thousand autobiographies, the respondents often mentioned another form of competition — the reading groups, each with a supposedly nondescriptive name. But the members of each group were never in doubt as to their level of ability. Often respondents recalled the names of things they read about: rabbits were faster than turtles, and certainly panthers could outrun and outsmart rabbits. However, the results of such grouping may have had positive as well as negative effects on members of the group.

Within the panorama of school with all of its new experiences, there are the memorable teachers, many of whom seem to have tried to make books and pleasant associations synonymous. Reading by the teacher is recalled time and time again as one of the special, fond memories of elementary school. Let us see what memories of reading are recalled by our readers as they move through the late elementary years.

Late Elementary Years

The first book I actually remember asking for was a book one of my girl friends had and I immediately put it on my Christmas list. I was in fourth or fifth grade. The title was *Pollyanna*. Christmas morning came and the book was there. By afternoon I had it read from cover to cover on even such an eventful day as Christmas. My parents were astounded. Now what was I to do to spend the rest of my vacation? I know I found something to be glad about for weeks.

As for every young boy, Christmas was an eagerly awaited day of the year. I could always count on practical gifts such as guns and trucks, and also, at least one or two books. I remember especially well one Christmas. I must have been nine or ten, when I received *The Swiss Family Robinson* and *The Adventures of Sherlock Holmes*. The entire family was home and the usual bedtime restrictions were relaxed. I felt unusually happy and secure as I began reading that night by the Christmas tree with the rest of the family quietly talking and admiring their new presents. I still remember the pleasant whirl of confusion in my head.

It is strange, but some of my most pleasant childhood experiences with literature were associated with times of illness. Actually I should be more specific and say those luxurious days of convalescence when everyone was especially concerned about my comfort. These were the romantic days of Sherwood Forest and King Arthur's pure and courageous knights — those wonderful days of fantasy and reality, the latter supplied by cookies and milk at the bedside.

In the fourth grade during winter I was stricken with a rather severe case of pneumonia curtailing all my plans of Christmas fun. Instead of being in the winter play, ice skating, and taking swimming lessons, I stayed at home and devoured as many Little Lulu comics as people would bring me. At that particular time they provided a certain type of companionship which I felt I needed.

All reading experiences at home were delightful and group oriented. Saturday night was a treat. We usually had pop, popcorn, and fudge and bought a batch of new comics for the event. We made a ritual out of munching and reading together.

Both of my parents read constantly and my five-year-older sister still reads more than anyone I know. Living with persons older than myself, I was constantly surrounded by books above my own reading level. As is probably typical, I always strived to appear more adult and tried to do anything my sister did. As a result of this, I diligently labored through *Crime and Punishment* in the sixth grade.

My tenth birthday was an important point in my reading career. I decided I had to be more organized. So I made the decision to begin at "A" in the fiction section and read all the way through.

Sometime during my third year in school, I found a book about a set of twins and their life in a small French town. That was the first of many books that I remember reading about twins in various lands. From that time on I read everything I could find about other countries.

It seems that almost everything I read during those years in some way was connected with the games we played in our neighborhood. When we pretended that we were knights, I read about King Arthur. The same pattern was followed through cowboys and Indians and commandos.

There I was sitting in our treehouse reading the complete, unabridged *Adventures of Tom Sawyer.* I was about in fifth grade at the time and I thought Mark Twain would've liked the idea of someone reading his book in a treehouse. Also, if Tom had read a book, perhaps that is where he would've read.

The most noted change in reading habits which occurred about fourth grade was my sudden interest in horses. I started a horse collection, wanted my own, and read everything from horse fiction to training manuals.

I fantasized for weeks while in my pioneer phase and settled the West, wove cloth and made soap many times over.

Later on came the Hardy Boys and in these books I found everything a young boy of ten could ever hope for in adventure, intrigue and the thrill of fast cars and powerful speedboats. My best friend and I often stayed after school to read books of this series together, frequently exchanging books. We always read with the assurance that virtue would triumph.

My earliest recollection of personal reading done on my own motivation was the Hardy Boys series. This was during fourth through sixth grade when it was fashionable among the fellas to read them. It was sort of a mark of prestige if you had read many Hardy Boys books. I checked them out of our church library on Sunday morning and would read solidly all Sunday afternoon so I could have it read before church on Sunday night. It was quite a feat for me to read it so fast and be able to tell everyone at school on Monday.

I thought the Nancy Drew stories were positively the most exciting books I had ever read, and truly did enjoy them. I even remember saving my allowance to buy each new book in this series as it was published.

My parents always allowed me to read as much as I wanted and pretty much what I wanted. They did limit the number of Nancy Drew mysteries and would never buy me one although they would buy me almost any other book.

At this particular juncture in my life I had a very good friend with whom I began writing a joint mystery. It was never finished, of course, but we were serious mystery advocates for about a year.

I can still recall the enormous stacks of comics which all of the kids in our neighborhood swapped from time to time. The arguments over who should get two issues of *Captain Marvel* for a more recent copy of *Crime* were often long and tedious, but many of the boys went home with more comics than they originally had.

Sixth grade was my year for the supernatural and it was made more special because I had a friend who shared the same passion as me for the supernatural. During the week we'd both read volumes. Then on Friday nights we'd get together and read the stories outloud. We had grown up together and one thing I remember best about this friend was that at night we didn't have to talk to each other, but could read.

I remember the summer reading programs and the little contests the library would have to encourage kids to read. One summer there was a "reading tree" and apples to stick on for each book I read. The best summer was when the prizes were little glazed plaster symbols of Iowa: a corn cob, a wild rose, and a shape of the state itself.

When I became old enough to read to myself I soon discovered the library and read everything I could get my hands on. This included most of the children's classics from *Tom Sawyer* on through all of Louisa May Alcott.

Every fall the big event in my life from third through eighth grade was the awarding of the book worm pins by the Public Library to those who had successfully read and reported on 15 books during the summer. This program kept me reading and reading every summer — so much so that my mother always had a hard time getting me to help her around the house.

My next recollection of formal school reading centers on the fourth grade when we would stand up and read orally and our turn lasted until we made an error. I do not remember the context of any story, but I do remember the thrill of catching an error and being chosen to read. Also, my dismay when I had to be seated because of mispronouncing a word.

It was about fifth grade that I remember being read *The Yearling* in school and loving every minute of it. Also during this period I remember thrilling to *Heidi* as my mother read to me to amuse me during a siege of measles.

My next positive experience of reading to the best of my recollection wasn't until fourth and sixth grades: both of these had one thing in common. We, as a class, were being read to. We were an audience. *Charlotte's Web, The Black Stallion,* and some others left me wanting to go back to school to feel more suspense, excitement and fun.

My fourth grade teacher read the books by Laura Ingalls Wilder to our class and nearly everyone loved them to the point of acting them out during recess. My sixth grade teacher read the Sugar Creek Gang series to us and we could hardly wait for Friday.

Then there was Miss P., a fifth grade teacher. After gym she would read out loud a book the class had picked as a whole. It was the best part of the day. And sometimes we could convince her to read more than one chapter. I still wonder what happened at the end of the *Mysterious Island.* I got sick and missed the last chapters.

Reprise

Gifts of books during these late elementary school years combine the excitement of receiving a present with the excitement of being able to continue a particular reading interest. Although some respondents may have received unwelcome gift books, they seemed only to recall the pleasure of receiving new books on special occasions. It is also interesting that, for some respondents, the periods of illness became pleasant memories because of books. Perhaps their pleasure was also enhanced by the extra attention they received from family members: back rubs, books read aloud, and special treats like ice cream and cookies.

During these years the family continues to play an important role in providing a model for the young reader. In many accounts, literature is associated with fun, as reading became an activity participated in together with other family members. Usually set up as a regular affair with favorite snacks, the evening became a special occasion. In this way, reading becomes part of the early socialization process.

Also, it is during these years that most respondents discovered some subject that nearly became an obsession with them. They read every book they could find, whether fiction or nonfiction. Horses, wolves, pioneers, airplanes, sports heroes — these and other subjects were pursued by young readers as were the standard classics for the young such as *Little Women, The Adventures of Tom Sawyer,* and other perennial favorites. Some picked up adult books, usually "reading" through them because they looked fat and impressive or discarding them after a few pages because they were dull.

Just as they read book after book on a favorite subject, the respondents also became momentarily addicted to both the series and comic books. Over and over the accounts describe periods where such books became their steady reading fare. The respondents shared them with friends and thrilled to the adventures of these characters who were larger than life. If you probe for the reasons for the appeal of such material, certain ones come readily to mind: they fulfill wishes, read easily, move rapidly, and guarantee a happy ending. Who cannot recall spending some happy hours with Nancy Drew or the Hardy Boys or Superman? These materials seem to be as much a part of one's literary maturation as are the children's classics.

When one considers the sheer numbers of the books that are available to young readers, it is not surprising that many recall their efforts to arrive at some kind of system for getting through them all. These attempts continue throughout the elementary school years. No wonder that these baffled youngsters usually settle on the simple plan of reading every book in the library beginning with the "A's."

Additional incentives for increased reading during the summer months are provided through the library reading programs and contests with their accompanying prizes. Some of the prizes that are remembered may sound familiar: a silver plastic brontosaurus, plastic circus animals, segments of a worm's body, holy pictures, feathers for an Indian war bonnet, and one grand prize — a square inch of land in Alaska.

An important, pleasure-filled school memory is that of the teacher's reading aloud. For many, it seems to be the single, most fondly remembered experience of these particular school years. (We think the concept important enough that we will give it attention in a later, separate chapter.)

Now let us look at what seem to be representative memories of reading and continuing to "grow" with books during junior high school.

Junior High School Years

> I did a lot of reading in grade school and junior high school, probably more than I have ever read since. My library card was

worn to a frazzle from almost constant use. During the summer months the library had a reading program in which I participated. After reading a certain number of books, a summary of which was made to the librarian as each book was returned, the reader was awarded a certificate and gold star. At the time, my certificate was a prized possession. In junior high or the early high school grades, one of the radio stations presented a Book Bandwagon program in which representatives of each of the schools participated. A number of books had been read and the panelists discussed these books on the program. I considered participation in these programs to be quite an honor.

In the summer following the sixth grade, I reached what I suppose was my reading peak. I read over a hundred books and sometimes four a day. At the time I made a list of these books which I wish I still had. I do remember such titles as *My Friend Flicka; King of the Wind; Cowboys, Cowboys, Cowboys; Indians, Indians, Indians;* and *Horses, Horses, Horses.* Positive books with adventure were what I mostly wanted.

My reading reached a peak when I was about thirteen or fourteen years of age. One of these summers I read over one hundred books and kept a record of number, title and pages.

True to the small Iowa town standards of my peers, at the age of thirteen I stopped reading. Sports and cars were the only important things.

In junior high and high school my reading as a pastime lessened considerably. Nor did I read anything on my own which had particular merit. I remember, however, that I liked historical romance novels such as *Gone with the Wind.* Actually, the one worthwhile interest which I developed in junior high was for the short story.

With the beginning of junior high school, my interest began to take two distinct paths. I read the assignments required by my English teachers without protest. They included the works of Longfellow, Whitman, O. Henry, and Harte. But at home I began to read my parents' books. I read these a great deal and with far more interest than I paid to my school assignments. *Brideshead Revisited, Tess of the D'Urbervilles* and a few of Shakespeare's plays seemed far more exciting than the things we did at school.

Early in junior high school days, I was a great mystery fan. I cleaned both the school and public library shelves of all the mystery books. In the middle of this mystery craze, I also developed a liking for biography and read a great many of these. Then later in junior high school, I turned to romance and only this type of book for the most part.

My horse age lasted until I was twelve or thirteen. Horse stories included the entire series of *The Black Stallion,* forward and backward, and *National Velvet.*

I remember the first book I read in junior high was called *Hot Rod*. I liked action and at this point in my life I was starting to get interested in cars. In eighth grade I read the book *Longshanks* (Lincoln's life).

While working on merit badges toward my Golden Eagle in scouting, I read many books on birds, stars, flowers, photography and stamp collecting. I can remember going to the Dallas Public Library and spending hours looking for books on these subjects.

In junior high I still selected books about girls my own age. My favorite author was Rosamund DuJardin. I read every book of hers that I could find. I liked career books, especially those about actresses, retailers, journalists, teachers, and librarians.

Since junior high obviously marks the onset of true maturity and adulthood, I found it now necessary to read fat books — *Rebecca, Gone with the Wind,* some by Edna Ferber and *Exodus.*

My seventh and eighth grade teacher, Mrs. T., interested the class in a book club distributing pocketbooks and I obtained most of my reading from this source. Books about science and adventure along with mysteries were my favorites.

Between the years of fourteen and fifteen, my horse stories gave way to boy-girl situations which also correlated with the social transition in the junior high school. I remember best the books of Betty Cavanna and the cloak and dagger adventures.

In junior high I read the books which we passed around school. They concerned either love, drugs, or teenage pregnancy. Perhaps it was then that I stopped identifying with the characters and situations.

This was the year (freshman) that I was satisfying my romantic bent vicariously. A few of these books probably stretched over into my sophomore year in high school. About this time, I also read books by Jack London and Arthur Conan Doyle. I also remember reading adventure stories such as *The Three Musketeers* and *The Prisoner of Zenda.*

My ninth grade teacher's words still ring in my head. She said that an intelligent person must have a well-rounded knowledge of books. Miss H. handed out a book list of books that should be read by the time one graduates from high school. This list started me off and it was a thrill to mark off book after book.

I don't think I liked teenage romance stories very much, because I remember feeling left out at times when other girls talked about the characters in certain series of these books. There were times when I read them, probably when I wanted to feel a part of the group, but I never could keep at it very long.

Junior high also marked the onset of skimming books — here the skimming was for "dirty" parts, each clearly indicated by the dog-eared page corner.

Candy broke me away from the innocent girl to the young romanticist. I guess you could say it shocked me completely, and I did the typical junior high thing — I hid in the attic to read it!

My sister and I always looked forward to visiting my aunt who had a subscription to *True Story, Modern Screen,* and *True Confessions.* While everyone else was involved in a 500 game, D. and I sat quietly behind the magazine rack and read as many as possible during the stay.

Reprise

By the junior high school years, when the reader is between twelve and fifteen years old, the process of reading has been internalized. It is no longer an effort. Young teenagers read avidly on their own. They talk of reading a book or more per day and of cramming summer holidays with reading. They enjoy keeping some kind of record of what they consume, so they make lists of titles, of authors, and even of the number of pages read. For some, gold stars doled out by a librarian serve as a sufficient reward, as do certificates or merit badges earned in the scouting program.

These protocols confirm statistical studies of adolescent reading interests. Horses seem a bit more prominent than dogs in the stories, but animal stories in general are popular, particularly in the early junior high school years. The great favorites are still centered on adventure, mysteries are mentioned frequently, and a great deal of interest in biographies seems to be developing. Undoubtedly, these biographies appeal to the rather naive humanitarian instincts of the young readers since most adolescent biographies are of the monumental variety. Teenage romances are of particular interest among girls. One respondent mentioned feeling forced to read some in order to keep up with her peers. Books about adolescent life, often mentioned by the writer simply as "teenage" books, surfaced in the 1970s and 1980s, but readers often move into reading popular adult material in late junior high school. Some make a concerted effort to be adult in their reading.

In junior high school, where English becomes a separate academic subject, readers often find a split between what they are asked to read in school and what they really enjoy reading. This can set up an adversarial relationship between the young persons and the school and may even result in the students feeling a sense of inadequacy about their own reading tastes.

The sexually explicit book provides another reading experience at this stage. Secretly, young readers pass these books around in a group, with the exciting passages carefully marked. Young people read with fascination the mildly erotic adult magazines and may be shocked by the details of some mature novels. But all of this seems as much a part of growing up as do the stories about sex that are passed along orally among the peer group.

It is interesting to note in the next section how the high school years show the writers' gradual movement away from an intense interest in self toward a desire to understand better the larger human condition.

High School Years

As I went into high school, the Ruth Fielding and movie magazine period was largely left behind me, and I developed enthusiasm for particular authors. I still have a tendency to read in this manner. I remember John Buchanan, Sabatini, Sir Walter Scott, Elizabeth Goudge. I read *Anna Karenina* and *The Brothers Kara-mazov* during this time too.

My teenage romance phase did not last long. As soon as I saw through these books and the popularity world of my classmates, I put them down.

When I reached high school I developed a rather strong interest for outdoor adventures in the far North. *Call of the Wild* was among my favorites. I read many stories about trapping and used to do considerable trapping on my own. At this time the average best seller held little interest for me. Generally I selected books that would increase my knowledge about some current interest. Seldom did I pick up a book at random.

Somewhere during my high school years I found Erle Stanley Gardner and Ellery Queen and I read everything by these two authors that I could lay my hands on until an alert and sympathetic teacher led me to "The Gold Bug" by Poe.

It was in high school that I found love stories. Most of them were from the public library so they must have been screened, but a few of us girls found *True Story* magazine to be most thrilling. The greatest share of this thrill came from the fact that we didn't dare let our mothers know we were reading these.

When I entered high school I was influenced by what my new classmates were reading and started reading best sellers.

In ninth and tenth grades my interest turned to biographies. I had been a dreamer from the beginning and I seemed to live with the people I read about. In later years of high school, I read a vast amount of material on psychology. I can still remember the librarian poking fun at me for getting special permission to use these books.

My shaky faith was made temporarily solid by *Quo Vadis, The Silver Chalice,* and above all *The Robe.* These appealed to me especially because of their historical background. I had great contempt for my fellows, but gained reassurance from *A Man Called Peter.*

I read *Life and Loves of Frank Harris, Jr., Lady Chatterley's Lover,* and anything else of that nature I could secure (and it was difficult — I met at once with fiery Roman Catholic indignation at home). I took special delight in perusing the drugstore book and magazine racks.

Finally I got my hands on one of those popular "What's Wrong With Nudity" and "Candy is dandy, but sex won't rot your teeth" magazines. Between exams in the spring (high school) when we all had lots of free time with squirt guns, and card games going, many kids each bought several erotic magazines and would pass them around. This was the thing to do.

In high school I kept "Annabel Lee" pasted on the inside of my notebook and *The Marble Faun* was my favorite of Hawthorne's books because of the aura of Roman legend and ruin.

I joined the Classics Club just so I could have some neat books on my shelf and pretend I was well read.

During high school I didn't want to be a conversational drop-out when it came to reading material, so instead of reading the complete book, I would go to the library and read the book reviews. I would also listen to other people speak about books and make use of their remarks about books as my own first hand reading experiences.

I read and hated *Vanity Fair* just before the James Bond fad hit me and I began stuffing my paperback collection with Ian Fleming's novels. Fleming was perfect. He had a "sophisticated" and dedicated protagonist who smoked, drank and did everything I wanted to do. Fleming also had an easy style to read and could describe cars almost as well as Ken Purdy.

By the time I was a sophomore in high school I was very concerned about being unprepared for college . . . . I had a list of classics and began my classics craze. I read every book labeled for the "college bound" student that I could find. I read many books that

I really liked . . . but detested others. I plodded through *Oliver Twist* thinking it was crucial to my literary development.

Then came high school and we future collegians began trying to read books on lists, books that we were supposed to have read in order to be college "material." Eventually I realized that many of the books one finds on lists are not worth reading and that one should follow one's own feelings in determining whether or not to put a book down.

With the reading of *Les Misérables* in the latter part of my junior year in high school, I began to see a whole new dimension in reading. Stone's *The President's Lady* not long after that helped to intensify the feeling that something existed in writing which I had been missing for these many years. From that time on I felt that I had begun to read as if for the first time. This was not the end of my growth, to be sure, but rather the beginning. It was some time before I was able to bring any real critical thinking to what I read.

By the time I reached my senior year in high school, Holt and Stewart had long lost my admiration. I felt a need for a higher kind of literature — something with "meaning." This trend of thought went hand in hand with that rebellious spirit which possesses the student around then that something better must exist or life is worthless. I took up reading J. D. Salinger, Herman Hesse, and all the far left pamphlets I could get a hold of.

In senior year I discovered Albert Camus and existentialism. These provided an identification not with particular people or an age group, but a less concrete identification with a feeling toward events and people and ideas.

My outside reading slacked off during high school as I participated in many different activities, so that reading, outside of the literature read during English class, was not very abundant.

I did not have much time for free reading in high school, for I was quite active in many organizations, dated a lot and worked as a waitress in a restaurant.

Reprise

As high school students, young people seem to become more self-conscious about their reading. They select their books and magazines deliberately rather than stumbling on them accidentally — just as they instigate happenings rather than simply waiting for things to happen. They seem aware of a definite change in themselves that affects their choices in reading material. It is as if they close a door on one kind of reading while opening the door to another. They are struck with an earnestness that launches them on reading the "classics" because their teachers or parents have led them to believe that this is necessary for college preparation. Some respondents, influenced by the need to keep up socially with a particular friend or with peers, make their choices according to the group. Others suddenly gain an interest in a particular subject area, history for instance, and read anything, whether fiction or fact, as long as it gives them information on the subject. Many others, intrigued by the works of a particular author, read all the works by that individual. Such authors are usually contemporary, popular ones: Grace Livingston Hill, Erle Stanley Gardner, Stephen King, or Danielle Steele. Few show a consuming interest in reading all of Dickens or Hardy or Shakespeare. Also what is considered erotic and therefore taboo has tremendous appeal. The forbidden books or magazines pass from one hand to another.

The most interesting aspect of this stage is that these readers begin to have their thinking challenged by the books they read. They come across revelations about people that are utterly new to them. They begin to see that authors embed a meaning in the action of the narrative. Suddenly, reading fiction becomes more than a simple, momentarily entertaining experience; it is seen as an intellectual activity.

College and After

When I graduated from high school I had just a little interest in contemporary novels and philosophy. In college for the first time I began to seriously question my fundamental ideas and attitudes toward life. In high school what I read seemed to support my belief; however, in college I was exposed to different and sometimes opposing points of view.

In a college directed reading class, I at last experienced sheer intellectual excitement. I learned to read not merely the printed words, but to appreciate Hemingway's attempt and success at achieving the fourth dimensional effect of writing, as manifested in the opening passages of *A Farewell to Arms* or Faulkner's playing with the reader by leading him like a dog and making him "bark up the wrong tree" as shown in his earlier works such as *Sanctuary*. The answers to the *why's* and *what's* became evident. What was baffling and bewildering now became clear, discernible and stimulating.

The tone of the book was very important to me, because I lived in the world of the book when I was reading. Only as I got into college was I able to enjoy books whose world was not one that

I would want to live in. Only at the college level did I begin to be able to see books as an art form, rather than only as new worlds for me.

Now what I look for in books is intelligence in the creation. I look for characters who are interesting, fully developed people, and who think. I look for wit in conversation and presentation. I don't object to formula stories if they are founded on sound characterization. I look for books that legitimately arouse an emotional response, and shy away from authors who do this unfairly by the push button technique. I look for precision and freshness in the use of language. I also read for specific information which often means that I can't ask for quality in the writing.

The biggest single event in my reading history occurred when I was a junior at the university — I became aware that what I saw was literary architecture and not just what I thought was a pretty house.

I have found a great deal of pleasure in reading, but until college I made little effort to discriminate between books. Therefore, I read a lot of "bad" books. But I probably could not have learned to recognize "good" books without them, and they provided enjoyment and fast reading.

On entering college, fiction and magazine reading was cut to a minimum. Most reading during these years was in relation to my study. At this time, however, I became fully aware of the immense value and pleasure that non-fiction can give.

We had read *Macbeth* in high school and I disliked it, for I didn't understand it. In my sophomore year in college, I read it again twice, once in a fine arts course and also in an English literature course. By the end of that year I decided Shakespeare really had something to say.

In college I look back on rapid reading of Wolfe, Hardy, Huxley, Orwell, Cather, Hawthorne and believe I was guilty of reading simply for the sake of reading them so that I could say I *had* read them.

I still have a nasty tendency to indulge in escapist fiction at the worst possible times — such as finals week, or the day before thirteen important papers are due. Pressure drives me to reading as it drives some people to drink.

While in the Navy during World War II, I read everything that I could find. A fellow officer's mother kept him supplied with books. I was able to read such fine books as *The Red Badge of Courage*, *Moby Dick*, and all of Hemingway's works, all of Maugham's works. The reading I missed in college, I made up for in the service.

The Korean War forced me to enlist in the Navy for four years. Here I had a tremendous opportunity to read a great deal, especially at sea. I held pretty much to the best seller type of book such as *The Caine Mutiny*.

After high school came the University of Colorado in 1951. Here was the carry-over from high school. I lost interest in any sort of academic work and with it went the reading. This changed after I enlisted in the Navy. There I read anything and everything. Most of these readings were of the pocket book type and I'm sure I read many of every type. My favorites were usually mystery stories one of which I would recommend to everyone — *Rebecca*.

During four years in the Air Force I read more than ever before and it ranged from pornographic paperbacks to classics, how-to-do books and current best sellers.

After college I joined the Peace Corps. While overseas I had the usual Peace Corps experience: lots of time and nothing to do. I turned to my book locker, a box of paperback books selected for volunteers. Here I read and reread Lawrence Durrell, Cather, Hesse, Kamala and many others. When I returned to the states I continued to read voraciously — Tolstoy, Dickens, Hesse, Michener, to name a few.

Since that time I have learned one important thing, which is organized reading. For instance, I have recently become interested in existentialism. When I read one book on the subject, I find other authors mentioned which I then read. Rather than scattering my reading I tend to read for a certain period of time on a certain subject or a certain author. This habit gives me a more organized approach and a more objective basis for judgment.

After marrying and moving to the Times Square area of New York City, my concepts of relevance and literature changed. I was overwhelmed by the power and ugliness of the American Dream. I read Eldridge Cleaver and Dickens and knew it was true. The suspended belief I thought necessary to understanding a book of human pathos was actually just experience with life.

When I was graduated from college I found it difficult to read anything pleasurable for almost two years. I don't really know why as I had always loved to read, but I think it might have had something to do with the fact that every time we brought up popular titles in English courses, they were ridiculed as trash and I somehow felt without realizing it that an English major only read certain books, that I was tired of reading those books and I therefore read nothing at all.

I discovered adult education and became a discussion group addict. I no longer wanted to read anything unless I could discuss it. There were several of us who belonged simultaneously to Great

Books, World Politics, Great Ideas, and Northrop's Meeting of East and West.

While pondering what to do after graduation I took a job as a waiter and read Thomas Hardy. I caught up on overlooked fiction such as both the Tom Wolfes, Kerouac, William Gass. I quit work the fall after graduation in order to read. For a month or more I competed with the Lincoln myth for eye strain. I read everything I could find by Faulkner, Fitzgerald, Hemingway and Robert Penn Warren.

It was in the army that I began to broaden my reading horizons. As it was in the army that I became seriously interested in reading, so it was in the army that I became more determined to write creatively. The more I read, the more I desired to write — there is no separating the two — to be a good writer one must also be an avid reader.

Reprise

For young people, college is a breaking out and away in all directions. Most leave their home and familiar community. They leave behind old friends. They may come to reject their old ideas. The walls of their world seem to be pushed back and may actually crumble. Reading now plays a double-edged role. It is at once a stabilizing influence inherited from their earlier years as well as the instrument or means for cutting old ties.

You will notice that the college-age respondents occasionally immersed themselves in old escapist kinds of books and enjoyed their earlier uncritical rapture. But more often, their reactions to books had changed. The protocols show that these college-age readers moved from a concentration on the content of reading to an awareness of how the authors handled the tools of their art: style, tone, characterization, plot, meaning. As they progressed, the readers came to appreciate those things they were not mature enough to appreciate previously in the great writers such as Shakespeare, Hardy, and Dickens despite teachers' efforts. The frequency of such comments suggests that it was not necessarily the teaching that was at fault in the secondary schools, but the materials. As high school students, many readers were not ready to enter the realm of the classics.

We know that we develop through childhood from an ego-centered being toward an awareness of the world outside ourselves. This development seems much akin to what happens to peoples' reading. At the college level and certainly to some degree in high school, young adults move beyond immediate projection of self into a book and come to understand experience that is different from and bigger than their own. Another chapter details more specifically the kinds of impact that reading has.

Later, the armed forces and the Peace Corps seem to provide a time of suspended living, perhaps a bit like a monastic retreat, in which reading becomes both the spiritual and intellectual guide. Then there comes a time when young adults desperately want a center for discussing what they have read, a sharing of ideas triggered by their reading, and they often seek some sort of adult group.

In college, freely chosen individual reading tends to be from twentieth-century authors such as Hemingway, (both Thomas and Tom) Wolfe, Faulkner, Barth, and other currently popular writers who may be less prestigious.

The protocols in this chapter, arranged in chronological sequence, demonstrate that the reading patterns of people growing up in diverse circumstances are remarkably similar. They move from nursery rhymes, talking animal stories, and comic strips to primers and the children's classics such as *Heidi, Swiss Family Robinson, Treasure Island* or *Charlotte's Web*. From the classics, which are specified by title, the readers next discover adventures and mysteries, animals and sports, and as they near their teens, novels about teenage life. There are fewer specific titles given about this genre, but the genre itself is clearly discernible.

Next, they find the adult popular literature. Although most readers are exposed to hardbound classics during high school, they do not really begin to respond to this body of material until college. And even as mature adults, most prefer reading contemporary writers. Here, they more often mention the body of a writer's work, such as Hemingway's and Faulkner's, rather than specific titles by these authors.

Part of what people read is determined by their cultural environment and the availability of materials. Interestingly, given the wide range of religions, nationalities, and intelligence that blend together in our citizens, as well as the widely different climate and topography in which they live, only a few of these respondents bypassed any of the common experiences that lead to becoming a reader.

2 Learning to Read

Learning to read is a pivotal development for most people in the United States. For some it never happens, and they go through life looking at reading and writing as an incomprehensible mystery. As adults, they find reading as baffling a skill as the operation of a computer is for others. However, in our social order, learning to read is considered the birthright of every citizen. We spend countless dollars on remedial training and professional guidance for the relatively few who do not acquire the skill at some point in their early childhood. The mysterious process by which symbols produce meaning should seemingly make an indelible impression on the mind of a child. But does it?

References about learning to read are scattered throughout the protocols, although this was not the subject the writers were asked to address. In the excerpts that follow, we will see some of the reasons why people want to learn to read, some attempts at self-teaching, and some positive and negative school experiences.

Preschool Attempts at Reading

Daddy never seemed to read me ordinary small tot's stories. Once he started to read a book about Richard the Lion Hearted and never finished it. He became awfully busy. I can't remember why, but I can remember the need I felt to finish that book. I *had* to finish it. I can still remember the feeling of desperation, of urgency I had. I can remember the look of the work: it was small but not thin, with a dark blue cover. I read it. I don't know how I taught myself to read, but somehow I did.

I remember wanting to learn to read so I could read the Sunday comics by myself. It was such a chore to get someone to read them to me.

I remember well the first strong desire to read that I experienced. This happened a year or so before I began school. My favorite picture books were copies of *Esquire* magazine and I recall viewing the pictures of the scantily-clad ladies, wanting most earnestly to understand the captions underneath the pictures.

My first recollections of any reading experience are of hearing and seeing adults read when I was very small, and also wanting to read just as they did. I used to imitate them by scanning over the lines in pamphlets and books. My cousins and I used to look at old catalogues and think that we were reading.

The very first things I can remember ever trying to read were comic books. I know I had comic books before I could read, because I learned some simple reading from them with the aid of my parents. I wanted to read what the pictures were about and what the characters were saying.

My first reading experience came at age three or four with following the words in the comic strips as my father read them aloud to me. I soon got to the point where I was correcting him if he skipped or mispronounced a word.

My first recollection of reading was the wonderful experience of having stories read to me by my parents and my older sister. My sister read to me from a primer so much that I memorized the books and by looking at the pictures I could recite it verbatim. Oh, the sheer joy of reading a book! Although I couldn't actually read, I think that this was the motivation I needed. I wanted to read more than anything else in the world.

My first experiences with "reading" happened in church, when I was around kindergarten age. Many of the hymns that were sung in Sunday School were very familiar, and more often than not, committed to memory. In my attempts to "act big," I found the page for myself or asked my elders to turn to the more difficult-to-find pages for me. Then, as the hymns were sung, I tried to follow the words, and sing at the same time. I got to "learn" words such as Jesus, love, me, etc., by association.

My first reading experiences were with Golden Books. They were mostly fairy tales with large print and pictures. I don't really remember myself, but my parents told me that I used to memorize the words as they were read to me, and later "read" the story while looking at the pictures. My parents thought I was very bright, of course, until they found I couldn't really read a word.

I can barely remember not knowing how to read — probably because I used to memorize nursery books and "fake it." My mother would read them aloud to me. Then eventually I'd "read" them back to her. Both of us know a surprising number of nursery stories by heart to this day.

My first contact with learning to read came with using the Bible. I had not yet started to school and I spent the long hours of the day copying pages and pages from the Bible with a dip pen on rough scratchy paper. After doing this for some time, I began to realize that these were words and next I began to figure out what many of them meant.

We were at the dining room table. Outside the snow was falling. My mother had broken toothpicks and made letters, then words with the pieces. Suddenly I realized I was reading a word.

My mother is and was a great reader. I can remember many times when I wouldn't know the meaning of words and I would ask her. She always knew. I also used to read the dictionary and encyclopedia. And still do at times.

I began my reading adventures with my older sister's rejected primers. I followed my mother while she hung clothes and stumbled over words of Alice, Dick and Jane. When confronted with a new word, I spelled it aloud. She patiently augmented my vocabulary. I finished this era by reading primers a year or two above my grade.

The first thing I can remember of my pre-school days as far as reading was concerned was that I received printed letters from my uncle who was in the service and my parents would help me read them and also help me write back.

Another early reading experience that brought me much pleasure was to be able to read the Burma Shave signs on our Sunday drives and infrequent vacations. It pleased my parents that I could do this and I also incurred the envy of my brother who was a year younger, but who had far surpassed me in athletic skills.

School Experiences

I can remember the excitement and thrill associated with the Dick and Jane readers. The teacher must have done a superb job in preparing the class for this experience, because the adventure has left an indelible image in my mind.

I do remember that at Christmas vacation of my first grade year, when my aunts who were school teachers in Chicago, came to spend the holidays with us. I overheard my mother say to them, "The child can read practically anything. She can even read the newspaper." With that I was asked to read the newspaper to my admiring relatives, proudly sounding out phonetically long words, the meanings of which — many of them and probably most — I had no idea. It couldn't have been called reading for comprehension, but in those days, it was reading — and for me an easy and delightful accomplishment. I don't remember any feelings of frustration that I couldn't understand the words. I rather think I had a happy feeling of accomplishment that I could sound them out.

When I finally learned to read, I was absolutely delighted. I would run all the way home simply bubbling over with my eagerness to show my mother what I had learned that day. She heard, "Look, Dick, Look" and "Run, Sally, Run!" until I fear I must have driven her nearly out of her wits.

I don't remember much about learning to read. We had flash cards, and my first reader was dark green with stories about Jack and Jane and their collie, Terry. If you didn't miss a word, you got a gold star in the back of your readers. After so many gold stars you got a blue dot. I dimly remember that I thought reading must be more lucrative than spelling where all you got was a purple grape in chalk on the blackboard or arithmetic where you got nothing at all.

I learned to read very quickly and enjoyed reading from the very beginning. In the first grade my teacher told me I was the best reader in the class and that I had learned to read more quickly than any other pupil she had ever had. I was always put in charge of the reading groups from first through about third grade.

I can remember sitting around in a semi-circle taking my turn reading to the group with the teacher choosing her students at random. I enjoyed reading at that time, and I always read with better than average speed and recollection — this is why, perhaps, why I enjoy reading today. It comes very easily to me.

In my primary grades, we learned and practiced reading by reading orally. The sound of words, the wording of ideas, the language of the written story and trying to read with expression were pleasant to me. However, I believe this much oral reading resulted in a persistence in vocalizing when I tried to do silent reading. This persisted even into college and was a difficult and slow thing for me to overcome.

When I started reading in school I thought that was the greatest thing that could happen to me. However, I found Jane, Dick and Spot very boring. Instead, I found refuge in *Winnie the Pooh* and a huge volume of *Mother Goose*. I don't think I'll ever lose my love for *Winnie-the-Pooh*. I can still remember the winter forest scene in the book. And what I remember most about the *Mother Goose* book is how I wished I could fly like some of the characters in the tales and look down from the sky and see lollipops and sugar plums all over the earth.

At the time (first grade) I was very obedient reading the same "See Flip! See Flip run!" and trusting it would get better. It began to bother me that the speaker was never identified in the book. Who was saying these lines over and over?

The basal reader was in vogue at the time and I remember hating to read aloud in front of my group. We were never allowed to read beyond the assignment by ourselves. One of our readers in first or second grade dealt with a definitely Catholic family who would stop and visit a church as they were driving to a picnic.

By the time I reached school age I was reading *The Des Moines Register* at night with my father. I thought it was great, but my poor kindergarten teacher was horrified. She insisted that I forget everything my mother had taught me and relearn her way.

When I got to kindergarten, the music and word rhythms of our language were exchanged for grim meaning in the form of maxims. The only reading I remember were short sentences of warning under pictures of distressed children. "This Boy cannot spell." "This Girl cannot paste."

Throughout the rest of my grammar grades I recall how frightened I would be to be called upon to read orally. Usually, I would read ahead and try to anticipate the passage I would be required to read. I was especially nervous when we were required to stand while reading. If anyone were to ask me about what I had read orally, I'm sure I wouldn't have remembered a thing.

By the time I started school I was anxious to learn to read. Dick and Jane seemed like pretty dull characters after my adventures with Sinbad and others. All Dick and Jane did was run, jump, and play.

Beyond this my memories of reading in grade school are mainly being told not to read ahead. As time went on, the word got out about me and teachers would come up on the first day of class and warn me not to read ahead. That is probably the single, most frustrating experience I had in grade school, coupled with the ridicule of other kids who thought anyone who liked to read was nuts.

A Few Horror Stories

Learning to make the sounds of each character and the combination of characters in the first grade still stands indelibly in my mind as my initial attempt at learning to read. I remember how the teacher mouthed each sound in a wild, exaggerated manner before we, in unison, repeated after her. Then followed the "solo" attempt. Perhaps this is why I remember this phase so well. It was because of that feat we learned. She stood near us with a ruler in one hand. Whenever we muffed a sound, she menacingly shook the stick in our faces and admonished hard, "NO, NO, NO. . . . SAY IT THIS WAY!" At long last in sheer exasperation the stick was used on many of us . . . I have no memory of the joy of discovering that "I can read."

As far as I can think back, reading was my greatest problem in school. I was always afraid and ashamed of my poor oral reading. My mother says this is because when I first entered the first grade, I did not know the English language. My parents spoke only Japanese at home. In the second grade I believe I was in the slowest group. I worked very hard in this class, for I feared the teacher.

About this same time I remember a series of very unpleasant experiences of reading at school. The text from which the stories came has escaped my mind, but the teacher has not. I have a picture of each student reading individually in class. We would begin at one end of the row and move down to the other, each pupil reading until he made a mistake. At this point the teacher would correct the mistake and then call upon the next pupil. I still recall the feeling of apprehension I had for myself and the sympathy I felt for those who always made a mistake in the first sentence.

The first reading experience which I can remember took place in the first grade. I could not read well. I had trouble recognizing words. Reading period was a frightening experience for me. I remember quite vividly a reading period during which my teacher slapped my face, because I could not read the book from cover to cover. As I read one day, my mother pointed to words here and there. I could not identify them. In order to identify them I had to count back to see which words they were. I could not read, so I memorized the book so no one would realize my inadequacy.

My first bad experience with reading came, quixotically, in the first grade. I sat in the reading circle and read the whole book while the teacher was still drilling on the first new word. Then I eagerly helped the other children over their rough spots until the infuriated teacher sent me to the cloakroom where day after day I cried in shame and frustration.

At this point (early school) I had a slight speech defect. The "ch" of words was difficult for me to pronounce distinctly. One day we were reading out loud in class and when it came my turn to read, there I was faced with this alarming situation. We were reading about "chickens" so you can imagine what happened. The class, as well as the teacher, burst out in laughter. Being the inferior little pupil I was, this was tragedy. As I recall, I "clammed up" for the rest of the year and flunked first grade.

I once had the fear of reading orally in the second grade. I can see Miss R. tapping her pointer on the floor as she waited for me to sound out some words that were difficult for me. She had already taken another pupil to the cloak room and spanked or switched him, because he couldn't read. I had been so happy earlier in the day, because I wore my new nursery rhyme apron to school. Would I have to go in that cloak room with Miss R.?

First grade seemed to exist only to indoctrinate me in the difference between home reading and school reading. Standing before my teacher, nervously pulling the elasticized band of my dress out until it snapped back against me, I can remember her words of warning about what would happen should I ever again read ahead and lose my place in the reading group.

In first grade I was punished by Mrs. K. for reading ahead in my reading book. She suspended my library privileges and took my books away from me for a week.

Upon entering school, reading — in essence learning to read — proved less enjoyable. I now realize the extreme importance of early school years in an individual's reading career. I well recall the frustration of having to stay after school in the first grade and miss a friend's birthday party, because I was unable to read a list of words the teacher had put on the blackboard. When the results of my first Iowa Basic Skills test came back in the third grade, my parents were convinced by my accumulative score of 39% that I was retarded and that my sister was the "smart one."

I cannot remember why, but in the second grade my reading was poorer than that of my classmates and I disliked reading. That summer between the second and third grades, my mother read with me for an hour everyday. I began to love to read. In the third grade, I read so much that I was not sociable with the other children. For this reason, the teacher removed all of my reading privileges and I was not allowed to read.

Reprise

None of the respondents' protocols reflects a desire for not wanting to learn to read. For most respondents, learning to read seems to have been a consuming desire. One reason appears to have been a growing sense of independence. Children still took pleasure in a family member reading to them, but as one says, she wanted to be able to read the Sunday comics by herself. Another recalled the frustration at not being able to see how a story ended when the parent became too busy to finish it. This is typical. There is a driving sense of curiosity about this mysterious skill that makes sense out of printed words.

Predictably, comic books were one of the first sources for self-attempts at reading, as the youngsters tried to figure out the meaning of the words accompanying the pictures. Another typical pattern was a child's memorizing a story read aloud and then pretending to read it. This was particularly true of material that the child demanded to have read over and over again. Others' early attempts at reading began when older siblings introduced the younger ones to discarded primers.

And some other first attempts included the reading of advertising signs on the highway.

Running through most of the preschool accounts are the models of adults in the family who read and of a strong family interest in and praise for the young child's attempts at reading. Sometimes older siblings were the ones who did the teaching by playing school and using their discarded primers as the tool. In other cases, adults helped find difficult pages in the hymnal. There are also those who would go it alone, such as the youngster who laboriously copied pages of the Bible.

Upon entering school, some recalled enjoying primers, such as the Dick and Jane series, because they were so caught up in the joy of learning to read. For most, however, the reading fare in school was a letdown when compared with the exciting materials that were read to them at home or that were already in the bookcase, waiting to be paged through. "See Spot run, run, run" became dull, dull, dull. The variety of methodologies mentioned by the respondents as part of the process of their learning did not succeed in making the learning experience pleasurable. Upon entering school, those who knew more about reading than their classmates were retaught according to the teacher's current method.

A frequent frustration was not being allowed to read ahead; some even recalled stern punishment for doing so. Who cannot feel the nervousness of the child pulling the elasticized band of her dress as she hears the teacher's warning about what will happen should she dare read ahead again.

By far, the frustration voiced most often about the process of learning to read was having to read aloud from primers. Some were embarrassed by mispronouncing words or were inherently shy and afraid of making mistakes. Others had trouble pronouncing certain sounds and were laughed at. Still others were bothered by having to put "expression" into their reading when they were already having enough trouble simply finding the meaning of the words. Perhaps, too, the child equates oral reading with a public performance at which failure is unacceptable.

A number of respondents recalled fear of the teacher. Perhaps some of these memories were exaggerated because the trauma of the incident increased with time. Certainly, the very newness of the school experience, when coupled with the struggle of learning to read, could produce bitter, frightening moments for a child whose early elementary teachers were neither gentle nor patient.

There were a few who liked Dick and Jane and who took great

pride in being the best in the reading circle. For them, reading aloud was a pleasure. Indeed, some respondents seem never to have encountered insecurities in learning to read. Praise from the teacher seems to be the key word in making the early experience a positive one. Although many of the respondents came from supportive home environments and were generally excited about becoming readers, they, too, felt frustration and self-doubt when they reached the stage where they were being judged by a person from outside the family.

In general, we found in the protocols an early, almost insatiable, desire to read that was stimulated by seeing adults read and by hearing stories read aloud. With arrival in the first grade came a good deal of frustration both with reading material and classroom practices. It was probably the personality of the teacher during these impressionable years that made the memory of some experiences so negative. Hopefully, the teacher who stands over the student with a ruler is gone, and children are allowed to progress at their own pace. And surely, teachers no longer suspend reading privileges as punishment for the eager child who reads ahead in the primers. However, some of these accounts of such punishment were still reported in the protocols written in the early 1980s. Certainly, the memories described here underscore, once again, the importance of having a variety of reading matter available to children in order to avoid the depressing contrast between what appears as exciting home reading material and the dull reading fare of school.

3 Literature and the Human Voice

As everyone knows, literature has had a long history as an oral art form during the course of our developing civilization. But the last two hundred years could be separated as distinctive from the earlier periods and labeled the "Age of Reading." Now, with the electronic revolution of the last half-century, the human voice is more and more becoming the medium of communication and the oral tradition seems to be once again ascending in popularity.

For some time now, there has been a controversy about the teaching of both reading and literature. Ordinarily, children's first reading instruction asks them to read aloud, to translate written marks into vocal sounds. But today there is a movement away from oral reading toward silent reading. Early on, children are encouraged not to move their lips in reading. Silent reading is, by its very nature, much faster than oral reading. Obviously, most people can consume far more material through the eyes than through the ears. After all, a half hour's news broadcast is little more than a column of print in a daily newspaper. Although elementary school teachers still read aloud to their students when time and the curriculum permit, literature teachers, particularly at the upper levels, feel that reading aloud is sugarcoating education. Young people ought to be "getting it on their own."

Yet, literature has sound. It has melody and rhythm and tone. And yes, it has a "voice." To read only silently is a bit like reading a musical score with the eyes alone. In the following passages, a representative segment of respondents describe their experiences with listening to literature read aloud to them rather than reading it themselves.

Family

As we rocked in the old rocking chair, I recall stories about the "big black b'ars," told by my carefree jolly Aunt R. During depression days a man and his wife picked corn for my parents by daylight and the wife told us children such stories as "The Teeny Tiny Woman" by kerosene lamp after supper. Several stories my Dad told as he remembered hearing them sometime, somewhere. My brothers and I were delighted to find a book in the

39

sixth grade of the Paul Bunyan stories that Dad had told us. Another favorite story my Dad loved to tell described "nail soup."

When I was very small, I remember Mother or Grandmother reading to me. I remember, too, that one of my very favorite books was Robert Louis Stevenson's *A Child's Garden of Verses.* "Oh, how I love to go up in a swing, up in a swing so high" still brings back many pleasant memories. Grandmother not only read to me, she used to sing stories for me — old folk songs and ballads — and I remember that the more bloody or mournful they were the better I liked them. When I was four, Grandmother's house became not a place to visit but my home. It seems that I was always sick and she used to read to me every morning, afternoon and evening to help the time go faster. It was at this time that she read me *Uncle Tom's Cabin.* I had been fascinated by the pictures of Eliza crossing the ice. Fairy tales and nursery rhymes were special favorites.

My mother rewarded me after I'd been good or cheered me while I was sick by reading to me. Many of my early reading tastes came from those sessions with my mother.

When Grandmother left us, Mother took over the task of entertaining me on rainy days, which by the way were my favorite ones. I'll never forget the terrible tricks I used to play on Mother to get her attention. One night she did not have time to read to me before I went to bed, so I started coughing loudly. Mother, fearing that I was becoming sick, came upstairs to check on me. Somehow, I convinced her that if she could read to me, it would relax me and I could go to sleep. I guess this has stuck in my mind, because I felt so guilty about it.

I must admit that my first memory concerning books was having my grandfather read to me by the light of an Aladdin lamp. When the evening meal was over, I'd crawl up on his lap and he'd entertain me by reading to me from a large red book. It was a collection of poems and short stories and to me it was magic.

One of my sisters was an avid reader. Every night she would read to me in bed. However, I kept falling asleep after a few pages and she'd become furious. I still remember the night I fell asleep during *National Velvet.* She woke me up and then threw the book across the room. I don't ever remember her reading to me again.

I vividly remember my aunt, who lived upstairs from my family and me, reading aloud to me *The Wind in the Willows* every afternoon after she returned from teaching in a nearby high school. I also remember — although this may be a bit nostalgic but true nonetheless — that during those reading sessions I was either in the process of eating plain donuts and drinking milk or pleasantly drowsing off to sleep. The latter occupation always produced a jab in the side and the retort, "Are you listening?" from my aunt.

I would live for the moments at night when my brother and I would lie snuggled in my mother's arms, traveling into the land of princesses and dragons and fairies, just by closing our eyes and listening to my mother's smooth, convincing voice.

One highlight was my father reading a biography of Elizabeth Blackwell aloud to me while I had the chicken pox.

My father also liked to tell us stories which he translated from Chinese as he read or which he read to us from newspaper clippings mailed from Jakarta. They were mainly Chinese stories set in Malay about historical, legendary or fictional strifes and heroes who were expert in the martial arts. We loved the excitement of it all as we lay in bed or sat on stools around our dining table, listening intently.

I was in the hospital to have my tonsils out and my mother started reading *Tom Sawyer* to me. It was scary being in the hospital and I can remember Tom's escapades as being a very comforting diversion.

When I was five we moved to a farm in Indiana. At that time my paternal grandfather lived with the family. He was an excellent reader and during the winters he would read to my brother and me. There are several books that remain in my memory. Sanpa was born in the Netherlands and enjoyed reading stories of Holland. I feel that my grandfather instilled in me a love for literature — but not for the overt process of reading.

I remember well one of my older brothers reading to me in my early childhood. My mother and father both read to me, but J., who was more than ten years older than I, was the one whose reading particularly delighted me. There has always been a bond of understanding between us which exists to this day.

Somewhere near the ages of five through seven, my father would read us bedtime stories and I was always play acting out the stories. I remember fondly *The Prince and the Pauper* and *Treasure Island*. These two stories moved me to mischievous actions. Whenever we could, we'd climb telephone poles making believe we were high atop a mast on one of Long John Silver's boats.

My father and mother, born in the late 1870s had their copies of their old readers, so we always read these stories and poems. Dad loved to recite his favorites: "The Wreck of the Hesperus," "The Spider and the Fly," "Maude Miller," "Battle of the Blenheim" (anyhow it was on the Rhine). What lines he stammered over Mother filled in. I still hear his voice ringing out as he gave such good expression to the words.

Teachers — Elementary

The teacher always read to us for about 15 minutes before classes began in the morning. During these all too short periods, I became acquainted with *Tom Sawyer* and *Caddie Woodlawn*. In the latter, the rhythmic words describing the wheat fields in the wind "bow, wave, ripple, dip" hypnotized me.

In the third grade Miss L. read *The Happy Hollisters* to us. I was hooked. I read every copy in the series I could get my hands on. I remember squirreling away change from doing housework until I had a dollar — enough to buy a Hollister book.

Our fourth grade teacher read to us for a half an hour after lunch everyday. I still recall resting my head on my desk and staring out the window into the trees while her voice created the day-dreams and visions of the stories in my mind.

Many of my elementary teachers had the policy of reading to us in the morning and at the beginning of the afternoon session. How I loved that time. I'd wait with dread as they turned each page for fear it was time to stop.

As far as fourth and fifth grade, fond memories remain of the books the teachers chose to read to us. In fourth grade Mrs. W. read to us from two or three Laura Ingalls Wilder books. At the time I was quite captivated by them as were most of the others in the class. In fifth grade Mrs. F. read a book which I've never since come across called *The Phantom Toll Booth*. It was a sort of fantasy story that I still think about now and then.

In one of the intermediate grades, probably sixth, our teacher read *A Christmas Carol* to us during the few weeks just before our annual Christmas vacation. I thoroughly enjoyed this work and I became most concerned as to whether we would be able to hear the end of the story before classes were dismissed for the holiday.

She would ply us through math and spelling with promises of reading time . . . . I remember wild flailing of small arms through the air: "Let me read out loud!" The chosen one got to sit on a stool next to that of Miss S. at the front of the room for the extent of one whole chapter.

Teachers — Secondary

During my seventh and eighth grade years, I chanced to have the same teacher and it was her choice to open the day's work by reading books to the class. She had the very fine ability of reading to a very exciting point and stopping for the day. Many times we would hold lively discussions as to what would be happening in the next chapter.

In eighth grade the superintendent was the reading teacher. He even read stories from *The Saturday Evening Post* to us. How I wished that I could read aloud like Mr. M. He read with a loud voice and always stopped at the exciting parts.

I do remember that my seventh and eighth grade teacher read aloud to us at Christmas. It was part of his Christmas ritual. We listened to Dickens' *A Christmas Carol* and *The Bird's Christmas Carol*. I thoroughly enjoyed this break from the routine and both of these stories bring back warm memories for me.

In seventh grade I had an English teacher that read Sherlock Holmes stories to us. This was great. I had always loved mysteries and these were of a new kind. They were exciting and he was such a smart man. I still love Sherlock Holmes and my favorite is the first story she read to us "The Speckled Band." This same teacher's husband read Edgar Allan Poe like it had never been read. He made several recordings and he could really make it come alive. He read to us and that was that. I read all the Poe I could and I even memorized "The Raven" although I was never as good as he was.

One vivid recollection is Coleridge's *The Rime of the Ancient Mariner,* which was first dramatically read to the class, Wagnerian fashion, by a robust nun. I later read and re-read this poem.

In seventh grade Miss S. tried hard to make the subject dull. She rarely read aloud and when she did she would sit on a straight backed chair in front of the room, too low for most of us to see her and in her drab voice, destroy a few paragraphs.

Mrs. K. made even *Great Expectations* bearable, her wonderful voice filling out Pip's absurd personality.

Believe it or not this lady (seventh grade teacher), a fervent reader of *The Chicago Tribune,* a paper she brought daily to class to share with us, read aloud to the class over a year's time Victor Hugo's complete novel, *Les Misérables*. As far as I am able to recall, the class — in its entirety — was held spellbound throughout what must have been a sterling oral presentation.

There was a memorable Saturday when I was hurrying to finish *Giants in the Earth* for a report, but my mother wanted me to help paint the living room. We had a delightful day by striking a compromise by which she would read to me while I painted. Of course, she became interested in the story, so while I rested and she painted, I had to continue reading aloud for her. Sophomore English was different.

The teacher was a terrifying French nun who could somehow

make Edgar Allan Poe and Tennyson resound through the class-room in unforgettable pictures and sounds. She liked what she taught .... I can still remember lines from *The Idylls of the King* and word pictures from *The Masque of the Red Death*. She talked about whatever she was currently reading or had read.

As a sophomore in high school, I had a teacher that calmly, with a Jack Benny like reserve, read our class Dorothy Parker's "The Waltz" and forever won my heart and influenced my ideas. I had never heard anything so hysterically funny and I had difficulty not laughing too loudly.

My senior English teacher didn't help matters any. She was an ugly old lady from Texas. She had two buck teeth and loved nothing better than reading Chaucer in Old English with a Southern accent.

Teachers — College

I went to a private college for awhile and had one terrific instructor who was an old Southern gentleman who taught American literature. He would read Mark Twain to us and it was incredible. Because of him I read many American writers.

In college my first English course was Introduction to Literature taught by an old man who would read poems and excerpts of stories to us aloud. That was when I seemed to catch an appreciation of literature. It was obvious how he felt about literature and his deep voice would float us along through the words.

I remember so well the beautifully modulated and expressive voice of Professor R. reading from the Bible and the *Agamemnon* and my own feeling of pride and exultation upon discovering the *Apology.*

Self

I remember how embarrassed I was when I mispronounced "island" while reading aloud. I said "is" instead of "i." Every time I read aloud now, I'm so afraid someone will laugh at me if I mispronounce a word.

I loved reading when I was in elementary school and I was a good reader. I can remember how proud I was when it was my turn to read in the reading circle and I wouldn't miss a word.

One of my earliest outside readings was the comic strip. I read these to younger brothers. I did this reading even after they could read well, because I enjoyed reading aloud.

Friends

> One night the five of us sat in Nancy's basement and took turns reading aloud from *The Encyclopedia of Murder.*

> That's when (first year college) I first met Ray Bradbury. My girlfriend assured me *Dandelion Wine* was special and I would enjoy it. She was right. I was captured by his style, imagination and the mental images I painted from his word pictures. Every day after lunch was reserved for a half hour reading and sometimes at night, though often I fell asleep. She was a good reader and certain parts of the story left hanging till the next day were exceptionally suspenseful.

Classmates

> Each day we would read one paragraph per person from *Silas Marner* round robin, saving ten minutes for discussion or quiz and would be assigned to read about ten pages as homework where we would begin aloud the following day. The long, drawn out study complete with plot and chapter outlines made *Silas Marner* the scourge of the year.

Reprise

The association of literature and the human voice has a powerful influence on a young person's interest in reading. We could have filled an entire book with the memories of family members reading to the youngster: mothers, siblings, fathers, grandmothers, aunts, and even an occasional grandfather. This is not to say that those who missed this experience did not go on to enjoy books. But such exposure greatly enriches early encounters with literature.

Some of the enjoyment is probably connected to the respondents' already pleasant, familiar relationships with the ones who are doing the reading. It is almost impossible to ignore the appeal of physical contact mentioned by many of the writers. "Snuggled in mother's arms" is a recurring phrase. Perhaps it is an association with the comfort and security of the home environment, rather like a family nest, which increases the child's pleasure. Sometimes reading is associated with food. Could this be the reason that many of us developed the habit of snacking while reading? A somewhat extended period of illness also seems to have been a period of increased oral reading for the child, perhaps because it passed the time and provided solace. At the same time, the stories, themselves, triggered the imagination and exposed preschoolers to elements of literature such as the rhythms and sounds of language — in short, helped in the development of youngsters' language growth.

During the elementary years, the family association is broadened to include the teacher. Over and over again the protocols indicate how pleasurable the respondents found the teacher's reading to be. Apparently, the teacher's talent for reading does not matter as long as the students get to hear a story. For some, it was the best part of the school day. For just about all, it was a time to let the imagination float toward strange lands and exciting adventures. We have included many excerpts because these memories were so numerous; they are certainly a tribute to the elementary teachers who make the effort and schedule time into the school day for reading aloud.

Unfortunately, the reports of oral reading by the teacher decrease as respondents progress through junior high, high school, and college. Oral reading by the teacher is still fairly common in junior high, but dwindles in high school and is almost nonexistent in college. Perhaps the teachers at the upper levels of the educational system consider it "babyish" to read to older students, even though most of those who mentioned an oral reading while in college did so favorably. There are only a few negative recollections, such as the Texan reading Chaucer. Obviously, the robust nun reading *The Rime of the Ancient Mariner* made a lasting impression on at least one of her students. Others mentioned becoming addicted to reading certain authors after hearing certain of their selections read aloud — Poe, Tennyson, and Dickens, as well as others not reported in these accounts. And let us not forget the professor's resounding voice as he read from *Agamemnon.*

Of particular interest are the accounts detailing the memories of the times the respondents, themselves, read aloud. Reading to a family member or friend seemed pleasurable, perhaps because familiar listeners are nonthreatening. The action is associated with fun and praise. Pleasure is also related to one's proficiency at reading orally. For one respondent, the reading by a friend had pleasant connotations. However, for most, listening to class members reading aloud was almost always dismal. Such works as *Silas Marner, A Tale of Two Cities,* and other classics were ruined through such activity. On the other hand, others of Dickens's works were considered good choices for oral reading.

Many protocols reflect a writer's fear and trepidation when called upon to read aloud during the early school years. Making a mistake in pronouncing words is a particularly humiliating experience, such as saying "is" for "i" in island. This topic is more appropriately discussed under the heading of "learning to read" but is mentioned here since it is an experience related to oral reading.

4 Reading Habits and Attitudes: When, Where, and How

Some aspects of living are more or less scheduled and become routine. Set times are allowed for eating and sleeping, schooling and working, and perhaps even for TV viewing. These blocks of time create a schedule for us. However, recreational activities such as sports and hobbies are part of our unscheduled time. Except for its use as a tool in school or work, reading must be relegated to this segment of our lives. The stereotypical picture we have of an individual reading for enjoyment is that of a person lounging in an easy chair in a pleasant room, feet on an ottoman, and eyes on the pages of a book. This is far from the reality described in the protocols, which are filled with vignettes describing when, where, and how reading takes place in the lives of the young people growing up in twentieth-century America.

Time for Reading

When I was about eight years old I used to lie in bed each night and wrestle with my conscience; I knew that I should go to sleep — but I wanted to read. Perhaps, unfortunately for my soul, my conscience usually lost the struggle and for several hours I would be almost lost in a book. I say almost, because I had always to keep one ear open for my mother's foot on the creaking stair, for although she encouraged my reading, she also had the idea that children should be asleep after eight o'clock at night. I learned early that if I tried to snap the light off when I heard her coming, she would hear the click. So I had to twist the bulb. This resulted often in burned fingers, and always in the feeling that I was a wicked girl to deceive my mother so, but the fascination of books was too powerful for me to resist — and has remained so until today.

And then came wonderful *Anne of Green Gables*. (Anne's problems became mine; indeed I became Anne.) I carried the book with me for "quick snatches" for days. It was then that I learned that the best book in the school room was the geography book, the publishers of which had thoughtfully made it a large one behind

49

which I could place *Anne* and just read away while the rest of the kids dutifully memorized the chief exports of Brazil. (I have never felt the need of knowing what exactly Brazil does export besides coffee.)

Imagine reading a Dick Tracy comic while others in the class were saying morning prayers! It's not that I was purposely impious. It was just that I was more eager to see how God helped Dick Tracy capture Flat Top than I was in asking my Guardian Angel's help in passing the impending spelling test.

If I went upstairs to fix the beds, I would pull books of adventure, books of fairy tales, *Mechanics Illustrated* magazines, *Boys' Life* magazines, old copies of *Reader's Digest* and even my Grandmother's nursing text books out of the shelves and boxes in my brothers' room . . . . When I helped Mother clean the house, it took an eternity to tidy the living room, because I read every magazine and newspaper I picked up. If Mother went into the other room or outside, I often huddled in the closet and read the old magazines stored there.

Reading! I read as many books as I could borrow. I read them returning from the library, on the lawn and the front steps, at the dining table (I lived in a dormitory), in bed in the reflection of the flashlight when lights were out. I even read while working. Doing part-time work for an elderly woman, I had to sweep the upstairs veranda which held a shelf of magazines and *New York Times*. Work went briskly until I reached that shelf, where browsing through the magazines and papers, I forgot time existed. A sharp call would arouse me, and work that should have taken ten minutes had required a half hour to forty-five minutes.

I read when I wasn't supposed to. I can remember lying in front of the heat registers in the morning when I was supposed to be getting ready for school. I was always late for school.

In northern Missouri during my first 12 school years, the women folk worked hard all morning cleaning the house or doing the laundry. The afternoons called for fresh dresses and time spent on the front porch. Since there were fewer labor saving devices than there are now, we found it necessary to make the best use of this leisure time. The four women in our family, mother and three daughters, made the most efficient use of the time possible by having three of us work while the fourth member read aloud to the workers. This reading was frequently interrupted between two o'clock and four o'clock when we all said "good afternoon" to our friends as they passed our house and by saying "good evening" between the hours of a little past four and dusk. It took me several years to figure out why people were unable to make an automatic distinction between these periods of the day. Stringing beans or stemming gooseberries was more or less painless when listening to *Three Men in a Boat*.

A Place for Reading

It was a post war styled overstuffed red velvet chair. As I recall that chair now it was really a large cushioned notch flanked by two perches which elevated my brother and me to mother's eye level . . . . Later, for approximately the next four years, I read a great deal in that red velvet chair.

I read in the bathtub, bus, bed, car, train, airplane, school library, outside, on the beach, on the sofa, on the floor in front of the TV (during commercials) and in my classes (and not always during reading time).

I soon became an avid reader in bed. I particularly remember the Sue Barton, Student Nurse books. At the time, good old Sue was my best friend; and she and I went through at least three typhoid epidemics together. I was also a "school bus reader." Being a farm girl, I spent about an hour and a half on the school bus each day. Our school buses were old, drafty, noisy, and had obviously been built before the days of shock absorbers. None of these slight inconveniences bothered me. I simply opened a book and shut myself in a different world. Occasionally I would read a sad book and end up crying sympathetically on the way home amidst a cloud of good-natured ridicule. As I look back, I firmly believe that I have my school bus days to thank for my power of concentration when I study now.

We had a room upstairs in our old farm house affectionately named the "junk room" for obvious reasons. I cleaned a corner of this room and turned it into my reading corner. Here I would sit for hours, surrounded by an ironing board, sewing scraps, toys and books. I liked these surroundings and have always preferred reading in a homey atmosphere to a public library.

The coolest place around our house was on the north side in behind the fireplace, next to the woodpile. There were lilac bushes on one side, honeysuckle hedge on another and a brick wall and the house on the other — people could come from only one side to see me. I used to "hide" back there. I remember particularly going there and reading a thick tome of Conrad's stories.

My favorite reading place was the top of a tall maple tree. My younger sister and an older brother and I would take a book apiece, climb a tree, play "monkey" awhile and then settle down to read where no Mother could call us to some neglected task.

Late at night I would sit on the floor in my bedroom and turn the book toward the hall light to read, forgetting the headache which this strain on my eyes would bring. During the day, Mother often couldn't find me, since I would be hiding behind some boxes in the storeroom reading.

A pleasant association I have with reading began when I was, I suppose, about eleven or twelve. My father built a seat in an apple tree in the orchard, and I can remember spending hours each summer sitting in this leafy bower, reading and munching crabapples or harvest apples. I know I read a great deal — probably too much. At least that is what my family thought.

Among the books which I enjoyed in the seclusion of the haymow or the attic, the latter an especially favorite place when the rain was falling on the tin deck of the roof, were *Little Women, Little Men, Rose in Bloom* and others of the Alcott offerings, *Gulliver's Travels,* etc.

Yes, it all comes back to me now — just as if it were yesterday — one of my earliest recollections is washing the dishes at the kitchen sink with a book propped up in front of me to read. As I remember it, I felt like a Cinderella, having to wash all those dirty dishes (my kid brother wiped) when I would so much rather have been lying out in the hammock reading my dear book. Oh! I had an unfeeling mother — a wonderful cook, but cruel!

When I was thirteen or fourteen years old, I was an avid reader and must have tried my Mother's patience when I propped a book up in the kitchen window to read as I washed dishes or balanced it precariously as I took a bath.

If bedtime rolled around and I was in an exciting book, I'd go upstairs and sit in the hall and read by the hall light. This worked until my parents discovered what I was doing and turned the light off as soon as I went up the stairs. I decided I could read by the light of the flashlight and did just that. This was fine until my sister discovered what I was doing and then I had to not only read by flashlight, but also under the covers so she could not see the light on her side of the room.

There has to be some fascination in reading by flashlight. I probably spent more hours suffocating under bed covers and in closets, and spent more money on flashlight batteries than anything else during these days.

Sitting in the closet, door closed, rug stuffed under the door and reading by flashlight was a common experience for me in junior high and high school.

When it was time for "lights out" in the barracks, we would go to the latrine, but read we would. I can recall a particularly fascinating evening with the novel *The Snake Pit.*

Sometimes there would be a book I wanted to read and a TV program I wanted to watch — so I would do both at the same time. I also used to read two books at a time too.

Systems of Reading

I began a list called "A List of Books to Read Before I Die."

As I recall now, if I found a book I liked, I would read all that I could find by that author. Yes, I'm sure I read all of the Zane Grey books. I especially liked Bess Streeter Aldrich.

I started to get books from the town library. I wanted to start some day at the beginning of the "A" shelf and read every volume to the end of the "Zs." I really expected to accomplish this, but in the mean time I found too many interesting volumes in-between to read first.

I would go on "self-betterment" campaigns and read a great many books of a particular author — Robert Louis Stevenson, for example. In the same way, I would read a great number of books on the same topic, like the Civil War. (I find I am still prone to take the same tack in my reading habits.)

There were small libraries in each classroom in our elementary school. I started at one end of the shelf and read every book. I ran across some losers along the way. But for the most part I didn't care what I was reading. It was an ego trip to read the entire library and I reached the point where quantity was all that mattered.

It is probably evident that I enjoy reading. I tried to read everything I could lay my hands on during the summer. I remember one summer I had run out of things to read around the house, so I picked up a pile of magazines from a friend. These were all cowboy stories. In order to make sure that I read each magazine, I would place a check on the cover. This procedure shows how alike all the stories were.

I did impose occasionally, some restrictions on myself. During the summer preceding sixth grade, I limited all my library book selections to that of fairy tales and Greek folklore. Another restriction imposed was the reading of only religious books such as *Jesus of Nazareth* during the Lenten season. Such a plan seemed much more sensible and positive to me than the giving up of candy done by my high school friends.

Food and the Reader

I always sat on the stairs reading (for some reason stairs will always be one of my favorite places for reading), eating buttered popcorn, drinking lemonade while my brother played classical piano records in the living room.

A chocolate bar, an apple, a Tarzan book and a perch in the crotch of our mulberry tree was all I asked out of life when I was ten. I can't remember if the tree helped to "transport" me to the wilds of Africa or if I merely wanted to escape my brothers and sister, but at any rate my book and I spent many a happy hour there.

As far as I can remember, my first recollection of reading was sitting in my father's huge rocking chair with my dog Buster, three jawbreakers, two sticks of black licorice, a peanut butter and jelly sandwich, and about ten comics.

I read in fields, in trees, in the barn, in my room, and for some strange reason whenever I read, I craved Fig Newton cookies . . . .

Someone was always willing to read to me until I was able to read for myself. These often took place under a dining room table, complete with jelly sandwiches, cookies and my great grandmother or great aunt reading to my cousin and me.

Self-Criticisms

I am an undiscriminating reader. I read anything available in spare moments, from the written material on the cereal box to the advertisements posted on the inside of a bus. I stop to read the times of pick-up posted on mail boxes each time I mail a letter, a habit my husband finds particularly annoying in that it is wasted and useless effort.

The weakness that disturbs me most seriously is my inability to read critically. I tend to accept the printed word as divine revelation. For example, I can remember reading two studies of the books of D. H. Lawrence. The first was highly favorable: all was presented logically, so I thought, and I was dutifully filled with admiration for D. H. Lawrence. Several days later, I read the second book, one that attacked Lawrence's books severely. This opinion I accepted just as readily as I did the praise of the first critic. It was only later that I began to wonder why it is that I shy away from the forming of opinions of my own. As I read, I read too passively; I read without a fight.

I always thought, as I still do, that I read too slowly. Consequently, I would push myself to go faster, but when I did, then I would miss some details. It has always been a problem as to how fast I can read and still absorb all of what is written. Now it depends to a great extent on the content of this material. I also dislike other noises in the room when I am reading something difficult.

I had trouble in 6th grade with reading, because I used to be able to read faster than anyone in the school, but had trouble retaining the idea unless I was interested in the subject. With an interesting subject, I had no trouble at all — I still find this true today. My parents got me a tutor who helped with vocabulary. I still don't know if this helped or not.

I have never been a fast reader. I suppose this can be attributed to one of two things; either I was never taught the mechanics of speed or I read novels in much the same manner as I read a text book. I tend to believe it is the latter. Details make writing interesting whether they be history or dime-store novels. I have always felt that I am cheating myself when I skim through a book and cannot remember details.

I have a weakness in reading — once I start a book I can't seem to put it down even if I have many important tasks that need doing — I will neglect school work until I finish the book.

I skim a good deal and only read word for word and slowly when I am either looking for some particular thing, or am enjoying a leisurely acquaintance with a book. I skim textbooks, then return and re-read sections of particular importance to me. I generally read very fast, and even when I try to read carefully, as when instructions are given, I am apt to come to grief; as witness my recent failure to see my name on a list of examination proctors at school when I had read the list four times to make sure that I was not on it.

My weakness in reading is the lack of speed in reading. I always catch myself going over the sentence just as soon as I feel that I did not really catch the meaning thereof. When I do, I read it carefully word by word which really slows me down. I know that I got this bad habit from reading too many technical books and not enough fiction books for general enjoyment. Finally, I am very weak in pronouncing new words, especially names of persons and places. The obstacle here is that I do not really know my phonetic sounds even if the symbols are shown to me. I do attempt the pronounciation of new words phonetically, but I am never confident of myself. If I do look up the word in the dictionary, I am not too familiar with the phonetic symbols; and therefore, I am still lost.

Since then, this matter of concentration on my readings has been my problem. I can sit for hours reading, but half of the time my mind is on the golf course or trying to bowl a 600 series. I'm glad summer session is here once again, so that I can "discipline" my mind on my readings and survive another six weeks of school.

I was a very thorough reader, but also a very slow reader. Somewhere along the line, possibly in my senior year in high school, I either read an article or heard a lecture (the source is forgotten) which started me on skim reading, and I developed the skill of getting the contents of a paragraph almost at a glance.

Reprise

Seemingly, individuals hooked on reading always find ways to tuck this activity into their daily lives. Certain times and places that they choose are predictable but others are startling. However, every protocol presented here was duplicated many, many times over in the reading autobiographies of other students.

It is not surprising that the summer vacation period is a time of intensive and extensive reading. An eleven- or twelve-month school year might not be worth the loss of summertime for reading. It also is interesting to note how many of the associations that are mentioned take place in the outdoors during summer. Still another predictable time for reading comes at bedtime. Both the place and time seem to cause a conflict between parents and child since sleep and reading are incompatible bedfellows. Therefore, the young people read by flashlights under the covers. They read in a closet. They read by a dim hall light while sitting on the stairs. They stuff rugs or clothes against the cracks under the door so that their parents will not see their lights are on.

Readers resort to still other forms of subterfuge in order to read. Some read clandestinely while supposedly cleaning the house; others read while a geography lesson was being presented; and still others read during a paying job. Obviously, these young people were adept at concealing the presence of a book they had chosen to read. Many reported reading while washing dishes; although this hindered their speed in finishing the task, the pleasure they found in their books seemed ample compensation. Other students reported that they read in the bathroom, particularly in the bathtub. One wonders how they managed this without soaking the book. The walk to school and the ride on the school bus were other times for reading, reflecting an almost compulsive need to read. One of the side benefits of the bus ride was the way in which it helped train the readers to concentrate on the reading material in spite of unusual sounds and activities around them. In some cases, a relative's or friend's house seemed more attractive for reading than did one's own. Other places for reading that were mentioned are the old-fashioned attics or lumber rooms because of their tempting store of discarded books.

Reading memories seem, at times, to trigger certain sensory experiences. Many protocols described reading in a tree surrounded by the sweet smells of summer. The eating of food is another delightful sensory memory: chocolate bars, popcorn, jelly sandwiches, and cookies. With these in hand and mouth, even hi-fi and TV did not seem distracting.

A number of protocols reported the respondents' concern with reading abilities. The students felt they read too slowly or too superficially or failed to get small details. As mature people, they became concerned with these seeming "deficiencies," considering them as possible handicaps in their future lives. Perhaps they were simply echoing what reading professors had told them about the present day's theories and, in turn, they tended to apply each condemnation to themselves.

Another interesting fact revealed by the protocols is the need for some sort of structured program for personal reading. The writers sought something more than a smorgasbord of literature, so they conceived the plan of reading every book in a classroom library or of reading library shelves in alphabetical order. More prevalent even than this was reading all the books by a single author or all the books on a single topic. In these self-set goals there is a certain amount of "oughtness" present. One person kept a list of books to be read before death finally struck. Others, spurred on by the approach of college, set out to read those works they would be "expected" to have read by the time they enrolled. Most of these lists are so extensive that they set up a physically impossible goal that results in frustration for the reader.

5 Sources for Books

Yearly, the publishing houses produce about 3,000 volumes that fall into the category of children's books. A walk through any large bookstore offers an overwhelming array of choices for young readers; the variety is about the same as for the adult selections. There are best-sellers, contemporary literature, and classics. There is an endless choice in nonfiction books from car maintenance to European cathedrals. The publishers have provided the fare. All that is needed is a population willing to spend money to purchase books. The participants in this survey probably represent that portion of our population who do so. It is possible that early availability of books helped to create the readers' need and therefore willingness to buy reading matter.

It is easy to surmise the conventional sources of reading material in our print-rich society — bookstores, libraries, book clubs, and the like. But we were constantly surprised by how and where, as children, the writers of the autobiographies actually found their reading material. It was not at all the systematic process that we had presumed it would be. There was almost a hit-and-miss quality in their discovery of things to read.

In reading through the protocols, it was obvious to us that, for many, the recollection of sources began in the preschool years and involved the family. We offer a good many excerpts from that time period because so many were given. Later, friends also become a key source, but we include relatively few of these accounts because their influence is discussed in another chapter, as is that of both libraries and librarians.

Family

> Our home was always full of books, most of which my parents had acquired at household goods sales. At the time when my friends were reading love romances, I was pouring through *Robinson Crusoe* and *Crime and Punishment*.

> Trips to Grandma's were also fun since she had a well stocked library of 25 cent kiddie books for her granddaughters, and my

great aunt kept 40 years of funny papers under her bed to delight us with.

I did it all on my own, since my teachers encouraged merely the assigned reading and my parents left it up to my teachers. My source was usually the odd assortment of books my brothers and sisters had gathered before me over the years.

From age five until I was eight years old, I lived with my grandparents on a farm in southwestern Minnesota. In his study, my grandfather had an oak secretary type desk topped with glass fronted bookcases. As a special treat I would be allowed to look at some of my grandfather's books. My favorite was a heavy volume containing pictures printed in black and white on glossy paper of sites of interest around the world.

About this time I also remember reading *The Five Little Peppers and How They Grew* repeatedly. Not because I enjoyed the book that much, but, believe it or not, because it lay with a variety of magazines in the bathroom beside the stool.

We lived in a very small town, population one hundred, where the only contact with books was those in our home. A monthly shopping tour to a larger town usually resulted in a trip to the dime store. We never left that store without a book.

I supplemented library books with books I borrowed from an old woman who lived in our neighborhood, the grandmother of a playmate. I would visit her after school (She was lonely) and she would lend me books. She liked to read too, and she had her bookcases filled with more books than I had ever before seen in anyone's house.

I advanced from my single book to a whole box of books that belonged to my brother. The summer after tenth grade I started reading books which were around the house — Fitzgerald, Salinger, Wolfe, Ibsen.

One day when I was home from school with a cold, I found a very old book called *Jane Eyre* in one of the book cases crammed with religious stuff.

One day I found four volumes of Sandburg, *The War Years*, among my father's books. I read them and subsequently everything else he'd written. I started a hardbound collection of Sandburg; I bought a bust of him; I drove to Cedar Falls to hear him read. I thought he was the greatest writer that had ever lived.

During my early years I read as avidly as my daughters were later to do — but with a difference. While they had an almost limitless supply of books from which to choose in school and public libraries, my choice was limited to our country school collection housed in an antique secretary and to the few offerings from our small bookcase-desk combination in the living room at home.

There was nothing before school: no ABC books at home; no evening stories from Mom, Dad, older brother or sister; not even newspapers. But in that first Reader, oh so vividly, I remember the story of the little red hen — and I *was* that hen: the story of the little girl who made the porridge that ran over into and filled the streets — and I *was* that little girl. I remember too, the story of the greedy, greedy old lady that turned into a red-headed woodpecker — and I feared I'd become that awful old woman.

In my first two and a half years of school, there was no library in the country school which I attended, so I did not have access to many books. Knowing that I liked to read, my mother purchased some books for me. The first three books she gave me are very dear to me, for they were the first books I had ever owned. These three books were *My First Book of Birds, Donald Duck Goes to School* and *Mickey Mouse and His Friends.* Though I didn't know how to read *My First Book of Birds,* I still thought it was a wonderful book, for it was something that belonged to me.

I learned to love book stores when I was still a small child. As often as the budget would permit, my mother and father would take us three children to a charming little book shop where we could browse and select our own books. I vividly remember the day I chose a book with a beautiful blue cover with a gorgeous picture of a pig on the front and many words on the inside pages. My older sisters laughed at me and I began to cry, because I was only in kindergarten and I could not read. My mother didn't think it a bit odd that I should select something besides a picture book and assured me that one day soon I would be able to read. The title of that book that brought me to tears is *Old Mother Grunter.* I still have my original copy.

There were four major sources of books during these years: the old books stored in our house; the library shelves in the little old schoolhouse that had been abandoned; library books at the school in town; and the shelves of books owned by the minister's wife. I hurried through chores during summer months to spend the day huddled on a counter in the country schoolhouse or retreated there during boring meetings of the Farmer's Union.

Near the end of the school year, I had spinal meningitis, so for several months, I had to go to my grandmother's farm to rest and eat lots of good food and get built up. Since I couldn't play, I read. My grandmother had eight children, so there were quite a few books. I dipped into practically every book in the house. If I couldn't make any sense at all out of the book, I would put it back and leave it alone. But if I could manage even a little part of it, I struggled through.

Books were not found in my parents' home. I must have decided
I liked books, because whenever we went to my grandmother's
home, I always rummaged through the shelves where some books
were stored. I read books that were not written for third and
fourth graders.

As the youngest daughter of a family of four girls, I can't remember
when I didn't read. I had started to enjoy books by myself before
I went to school. Never can I recall any direction from my family
as to what I should read or whether the material was appropriate
for my age or would enrich my experiences. I read what I wanted
to or simply selected available books that were being enjoyed by
members of my family. My home had a good library with many
periodicals. It was natural to pick up books and magazines. The
monthly arrival of *St. Nicholas Magazine* and *Youth's Companion*
were days of anticipation, but equally so were the delivery dates
of adult magazines.

Gifts

My first book that I remember was given me by my aunt when
I was about seven. I have never read it. I can remember when I
tried to read it I couldn't go on. I now think the style was so
formal and the vocabulary beyond my understanding. I prized it
for what it stood for — a book of my own. I know I had nursery
rhyme books before this, because I knew them at an early age.
My mother had been a rural school teacher and she read them
to me at the close of the day while we waited for father to finish
the chores.

As a youngster, I was always encouraged to read through gifts of
books. A feeling of obligation always accompanied such gifts, a
fact which contributed to my writing a book report from Monarch
Notes of *Moby Dick* in high school after I found it uninteresting
at an earlier age. I had felt that I just couldn't waste the time on
this book, so I got around it in this way.

One day I remember I was the happiest kid ever on Christmas
day. I had gotten two books — one from Mom and the other from
Dad. I read and reread these books.

At seven, I was given a Bible story book by my grandmother and
then a ten cent copy of *Grimm's Fairy Tales* from a second hand
store. They brought immeasurable joy.

Books Discovered by Accident

After I discovered the bookcases in the third floor attic room, I
spent many afternoons there reading. It was a varied collection

left behind by aunts and uncles when they moved away from home.

In seventh and eighth grades I devoured every copy of *Reader's Digest* I could find out of a huge collection in my grandmother's attic, and among the most avidly read were those sections on sex and marriage, usually shared with a girl friend.

For awhile I was reading old, old *Big Little* books someone had unearthed in an attic, vintage 1940's.

I discovered most of my reading at one time in the attic, in boxes of books my mother had stored there.

Our family had acquired some books from the attic of a house into which we moved. Though I didn't read the books in their entirety, I vividly remember leafing through again and again two big books, one about the Johnstown flood and the other, the sinking of the *Titanic*. It was through this means that we acquired many Horatio Alger books. I read them all, but recall my teacher would give me credit for only one.

I suppose the most traumatic experience of my young life took place on a visit to Des Moines when I was in ninth grade. For once we were allowed to go to a second hand book store, my first time, and I found what a magnificent thing is the dust which seems to swaddle old books in a properly dusty book store.

During my grade school years, I especially looked forward to summer. My father was a director of a rural school. One of the duties of the director was to put all the library books in a big box and keep them for the summer. The books were old and dusty, but I enjoyed them.

It was the summer following my graduation from the eighth grade that the world of books really opened to me. The school was just above my home and it was my job to carry water from the school cistern to my home on wash days. I had seen the old high school library which was no longer used, because the high school had been moved to another and more modern building. On my first trip to get wash water that summer, I went up to the old library and looked at the books. I remember approaching the rows of books with fear and trembling. I took two bucketsful of books out and stacked them in the middle of the elderberry patch. After carrying the water, I raced back to the books and proceeded to read. I sneaked often to the elderberry patch that summer, because my father was opposed to my reading and I had to keep it secret. The heavy warmth, the sweet smell of the summer grass, the trembling shade of the elderberry leaves — all of these are part of the memories of this period of my reading.

I was now in high school. I had forsworn *Hot Rod*, *Car Craft* and the works of Felsen. I was reading *Car and Driver* and the books of Ken Purdy and looking for something else. I found it, but not when I was looking for it. I was downtown with a friend and we stopped to see his girlfriend. He and she began what was to be a long necking session. I picked up the book she had been reading and went into the kitchen — *Animal Farm*. I realized what I was reading but couldn't describe it as satire. I liked it, so I read *1984*, and then *Brave New World*.

Once in the deep jungle of New Guinea, we found a little library of some missionary in ruins. Each of us got one book. I got the biggest one I could find which was *A Short History of Civilization*. I read it over and over.

Teachers

There were, however, a number of books in a little case in the hall. The teacher of the sixth, seventh, and eighth grades had put them there and they must have been given to him by someone. The books were available and I took them home and read them. The ones I remember are *Don Quixote, The Autobiography of Benvenuto Cellini*. There was also a book by Gauswitz on the tactics of war and a play by Goldsmith, *She Stoops to Conquer* among the books. *Little Women* was there and another called *Little Men* and yes, a book titled *Little Lord Fauntleroy*.

My intermediate teacher brought boxes of books into the schoolroom. We children could browse them at our leisure and read to our heart's content. This was when I read *Black Beauty, Robinson Crusoe, Beautiful Joe* and *The Pony Boy Riders*.

Fortunately my mathematics teacher brought me a box of her college paperbacks which made me very happy.

Friends

When I was about nine or ten years old I was given a series of paperback books by a boy in our neighborhood who was moving to another city. Why he gave them to me, I'll never know, but they contributed a great deal to my early interest in reading. It was with this series of short stories, abbreviated biographies and shortened sketches of historical events that I first did any reading on my own.

A friend of mine had almost all the Nancy Drew stories that were out at the time and we used to spend hours in her room reading and rereading them. I bought those she didn't have — or those that were my favorites. My aunt had the entire collection of Cherry

Ames, Nurse books — except for some of the newer ones — and I read those as well.

The first really vivid memory I have of reading a specific type of book is tied closely with the memory of a little girl I used to play with. Her family lived on the same block as we did, but they were kind of outcasts in the neighborhood. They were uprooted Ozark hill folk in an area of very middle class suburbia. But differences didn't matter much to us then and I spent most of my free time over there. What made this family especially intriguing was that they all (adults included) read comics. While we were only able to buy comics when we saved enough from our allowances, they had actual subscriptions to many different comics.

Somewhere around sixth grade, I started reading *Seventeenth Summer, Fifteen* and an unending supply of such books. A friend had a supply and I borrowed each and every one. Another friend had a whole supply of Nancy Drew books, so I read all those. Likewise, my brother's friend had all the Hardy Boys, so I read all those.

One summer between seventh and eighth grades or eighth and ninth grades, I purchased a huge box of boys' books from my neighbor. There were about forty or fifty books in it and in the next summer and year following, I must have read them all: *Tom Swift, Circus Dan, The Boy Scouts, The Submarine Boys*, stories of the barnstorming Flying Jinny era and many more of this type.

Our local druggist would tear the cover from old magazines and stack these issues on the front step of the drug store. First one there could cull through and take what he wished. I was soon initiated to *True Romances,* but Mr. Moffitt saw me choose this type of pulp magazine and took the opportunity to deliver a lecture on good literature. The small town was interested in educating the "motherless twins." He invited us to come to his house for additional books. Though we didn't realize the generosity of his offer, we were soon exposed to the treasures of a lifetime of reading.

Outgrowing Mother's books and being inquisitive, I began during the seventh grade to borrow books and magazines from older girlfriends whose parents either didn't know or didn't care what kind of literature their daughters read. With an adolescent's normal interest in sex, I read such trash as *True Story* magazines and books of a similar nature.

Starting in the fourth grade, I always ordered books from Scholastic Book Services. This and the small shelf of books in the classroom served as my main source of reading material.

We also had a book club at school where you ordered paperback books. I never missed buying at least two books each time and I should add that I bought these books out of my allowance. I used to do special jobs for Dad just so I could buy more books.

I was always in a reading program of some kind. My parents joined the Weekly Reader Book Club for me every year I was in elementary school.

In junior high I was able to buy paperback books through the Scholastic Book Club. During this period I read many, many adolescent romances.

One great thing that happened in my junior high days was the Teenage Book Club. I got a great start on a paperback collection that way and also got started on many classics, plus a lot of pleasant escapist fiction.

Reprise

Apparently, the kind of reading material found around the house is unimportant. What is important is that there *be* some reading material. The budding reader will pick up just about anything wherever it happens to be accessible — on a dusty bookshelf, an oak secretary, a rack in the bathroom. It is interesting to note how many of the participants in the study associated trips to grandparents' homes with the discovery of books.

Times of idleness also seem to encourage exploration. Summer vacations or illness may create a sense of boredom that can lead the young person to seek something to do. Sometimes that means discovering a book around the house or being given gift books. Remember the person who "dipped" into practically every book in his grandmother's house during recovery from meningitis?

A particular thrill seems to come from books that are chanced upon. Imagine the enchantment felt by that individual who found the little library in the ruined mission in the jungle of New Guinea. For many, attics and basements were gold mines. There seems to be a sense of adventure in unearthing dusty volumes, the older and dustier, the better. Boxes of books, whether brought in by a teacher or bought from a neighbor, give the recipient the sense of opening a treasure chest. One important point is that these books offer the young reader some choices. Some may read every book, but all have a sense of freedom, for they can try anything and reject anything without explanation to an adult. Choosing what to read from the abandoned books is a bit like choosing from among several flavors of popsicles.

The family, of course, is a rich source for reading fare in the form of hand-me-downs — from siblings, cousins, aunts, and uncles. Trips to a store, often with a parent, to buy a book also provide good memories, springing in part from a special sense of ownership. Many writers in this study recalled treasuring and rereading books given as gifts. There is probably an association of affection, here, toward the giver, as well as in the pride of ownership. One writer even recalled not being able to read the gift book but took her pleasure just in owning it.

It is a popular assumption that children from middle- and upper-class homes with educated parents have a head start on others in becoming better students and developing an early interest in reading. Perhaps this idea stems from the belief that such families can afford more reading material to stimulate the child's interests. This may be a valid assumption, and since we have no breakdown on the socio-economic backgrounds of this study's participants, we cannot challenge it. Still, many of the respondents' recollections indicated that they were not from reading families, their parents were not educated, and their homes were far from well-to-do. Some of those are given here, but there were many others in the thousand-plus autobiographies. Some parents were poor, but the few books at home were treasured and read and reread. In other cases, although it was a strain on the budget, parents took the family to a store and permitted each to buy a book. Whether it was a dime store or the books were old or secondhand, money was found for these purchases. The fact that parents placed value upon providing a book source was important in creating a reader.

Certainly, not all parents had a formal education. One youngster spent most of her spare time with an Ozark hills family, all of whom read masses of comics. Others reported that they came from immigrant families with parents who had little education. Still, they read something, if only newspapers, so that the child saw adults as reading people.

The book clubs are another source reported in the autobiographies. These, too, offered both freedom of selection and the joy of ownership. The young reader who looks forward to the catalogue of Scholastic Book Club selections and earns or saves enough money to buy selections is beginning, hopefully, a lifelong habit. There is nothing that indicates that those who were simply given money for the purchases did not also gain similar benefits from this kind of book source. It appears that ready access to reading material at a young age is an important factor in creating adult readers, whether the family is poor or comfortably situated.

While most of the protocols indicate the availability of some reading matter from *Reader's Digest* to the classics, we cannot forget the account of the eighth grader who took a bucketful of books from an abandoned high school library on his trips to a cistern for water and secretly read them in the elderberry patch because his father opposed his reading. There are some, like this individual, who will find books regardless of obstacles. But how much richer the earlier years might have been had reading been encouraged and books been made accessible.

The sources reported in these protocols are ones that could be expected. But it is the unusual experiences that are intriguing and reveal how haphazard and capricious are the events that lead to the meeting of the young with reading material. One begins to wonder whether the lack of attics and basements in modern housing will be a handicap in creating the readers of tomorrow. Are there still places where discarded books can be stored in apartments and houses to be found at some later date by an incipient reader? Or must America find a new way of nurturing reading for the young?

6 Reading and Human Relations

Much has been written about literature's potential in developing human understanding. A book can provide a reader with information, insights, attitudes, experiences, or emotions. A subsequent chapter provides ample evidence that such does happen to our readers. But running through the autobiographies was another facet of reading and its effects on the readers. Books seemed to serve as a kind of catalyst in social interactions between the reader and other people. The activity of finding books, the talking with others about the ideas they spawned, and the critical analysis of their truths and the craftsmanship therein seemed catalysts for social interaction.

Family Influence

In thinking back to the time before my tree-reading days, I can recall vividly two different emotions about stories. One feeling was a happy one which I felt each time I climbed into my father's lap and begged for a story. He always obliged and I'd begin it for him by saying, "Once ponce a time . . . ." He told me fairy tales and nursery stories, but the best stories of all were his original ones . . . sort of Arabian Nights fantasies complete with flying carpets. My other emotion was a feeling of frustration which I'd feel when everyone in the family sat down to read. I am told I'd hold a book to my eyes at such times and say, "Read, read," over and over. I do remember how badly I wanted to learn to read.

My father would lie on his stomach on the bed with his head hanging over the edge reading our set of blue encyclopedias and I would lie on his back and hang my head over his shoulder and read with him.

I was reared on an Iowa farm and attended a one room rural school. My life was as full of reading experiences as was possible at that time. My father never sat down to rest that he did not have some reading material. Long before I was old enough to attend school, I vividly recall that Mother read to us in the evenings and always on Sunday afternoons, and how we did look forward to these family sessions.

As a small child, I did not have access to as much reading material as I would have liked, although we were considered a bit unusual by our neighbors in at least one respect; my father always subscribed to a daily paper, several farm papers, and some periodicals.

Around this time (5th grade) I was very impressed with *The Island of the Blue Dolphins*. I excitedly recommended it to my father and I asked him to read it. He read it and only now do I realize how considerate he was in reading it and letting me share it with him.

My father probably influenced my reading the most — at least on an overall and importance kind of scale. I once asked him what he read as a boy and then went on to read what he had read. I read all the Leather Stocking Tales with Natty Bumpo, all of Robert Louis Stevenson's adventure stories. Even Dickens held my fancy long enough to get a sampling.

I would also like to point out my whole family's interest in detective stories. Of my father's personal library of nearly 2,000 books (of which about 300 are mysteries) I have read all of the mystery books and about half of the others.

I was a tomboy at this age and a worshipper of my older brother. Therefore I began reading sports stories: first about basketball. When I exhausted basketball, I began on football. I remember only two titles: *The Iron Duke* by Tunis and a biography of Knute Rockne which was far and away my favorite book of the sports stage.

My brother spent so much time lounging about reading his books that I began wondering what was so fascinating about them. After some persuasion, he agreed to let me read some of the books as he finished them. These were my first experiences of wanting to and enjoying reading on my own.

During grade school days, my sister and I each checked out three library books a week (library limit) and then traded with each other so that we'd have enough to read to last the week. Each fall we had to report how many books we'd read during the summer, but I never gave a true estimate because I was ashamed to say I had read almost one hundred books while some students had read none.

Literature was an integral part of my childhood with always my older sisters leading the way at home. Through them I was introduced to my favorite high school author, Dorothy Canfield Fisher. Others to whom I was partial included Willa Cather, Jane Austen and Thomas Hardy.

My parents were divorced; I lived with my mother who worked all day. The only human relationship I actually craved was that of my cousin, seven years my senior. To be accepted by A. I had to do as she did. This meant, among other things, reading the same books she proposed to read. And so, instead of *Little Women*, *Jane Eyre*, and *Black Beauty*, I feasted upon *A Farewell to Arms*, *Gone with the Wind*, and *Brave New World*. You can imagine how shocked I was to learn how eventually children would be born in test tubes, reared not by parents, but rather by assigned nurses. My bewilderment grew even more when I read of a "controller" whose duty it was to insure each man's permanent continuance on an assigned job.

Friends and Their Effects on Reading

Early Years

When I was in second grade a new girl moved into our neighborhood. She had more books than I ever dreamed of owning and I read every one of them. All of the Bobbsey Twins, the Sue Barton books, *Hans Brinker or the Silver Skates*, and the whole series of Rudyard Kipling's *Just So Stories*.

I seem to recall that when I first started to read a lot of books it was because I was competing with a friend of mine whom I thought was very smart. We kept a list of all the books we read and compared the list to see who had won for the week. After I moved away from my friend I realized that I had acquired a love of good books and also a love of writing.

I was given *The Wizard of Oz*. It is so worn out that it hardly hangs together anymore. Every kid in town read it. It got lost. Turned up when my best friend, Tilly, helped her family clean house. Then it started the rounds again.

We had a good many books at home and I had a friend who had a good library. We exchanged books and enjoyed talking about our reading.

I read these along with my best friend who lived next door and we would exchange books. We read from the time we got home from school — usually in Susan's bedroom until the time my mother called for me to set the table.

Because my friend was interested in nursing, she and I read all of the Sue Barton series.

At this time also, I became good friends with a girl who owned horses. She taught me to ride reasonably well and we rode for miles every Saturday. We began reading together also and the books we chose were inevitably horse and dog stories.

Another influence on my early reading was the Methodist Presiding Elder, Brother S. Whenever he came to town for a quarterly conference, he always ate dinner at our house. After he had eaten all the soft biscuits he wanted, he would talk to us all about books. He would buy books in the second hand book shops in A. and send them to my family. When the box arrived I could hardly wait to get it open. There would be books for everybody in the whole family.

High School Years

At about the same time (junior high) I decided to read the Bible because a friend was making a habit of reading a chapter every night. I got through Genesis and quit.

I particularly remember spending the hot summer days of the year after I finished eighth grade reading. I was visiting my aunt and became close friends with a girl my age who, although quite a tomboy, had a streak of romanticism and we spent long afternoons reading and talking. We also had some fascinating discussions. *The Three Musketeers* appealed to us very much. These lazy days remain quite a happy memory.

My friends were really the push I had for reading. My best friend read the encyclopedias for fun! She introduced me to many highbrow books and poetry. I imagine we were some of the few seventh graders that had read *Candide* twice.

Somewhere about this time (eighth grade) I became quite close to a girl whose older brother was an avid reader. We tended to idolize him and we both were strongly influenced by his reading tastes.

It became the fad for a while for us girls in highschool to discuss our reading at lunch time or any other free time we had.

My experience with the book *Hot Rod* is an example of my being influenced by my peer group. I passed this book up several times because I was not interested in cars or driving at this time; but after repeated contacts with the book, I finally broke down and read it.

One of my friends happened to see a copy of Colin Wilson's *Violent World of Hugh Greene* at the library and since she liked the picture of him on the dust jacket she checked it out. That's how our Colin Wilson kick got started.

I tried to keep up on current literature and books lists and began to again use the library. I would get this "good feeling" when someone mentioned a book that I had read (I still do). I felt proud to be able to recognize a book being spoken about and able to participate in the discussion of a book I had read.

By then (high school) word had been received from previous

graduates home from college of what one should and would be reading. *Lord Jim* at one private Indiana college was a must, Steinbeck at Illinois and so on. We bandied "great writers" about whether we had read them or not.

When I was a senior in high school, I began to expand my reading interests. One of the main reasons for this was my "steady," who was a very brilliant, well-read young man. We read and discussed Shakespeare, Aeschylus, various philosophers and poets and even Freud. We would get interested in a certain topic such as mental telepathy or Thomas Mann and study them for a few weeks, although I must admit that he furnished most of the ideas while I acted as a sponge.

Reading really began to interest me while teaching swimming at a camp the summer of graduation from high school. My guide was a marvelous girl who had had two years of college already and with whom I worked. That summer she convinced me that reading can be fun and led me to good literature. First I read *The Ugly American* and then *To Kill A Mockingbird, Catcher in the Rye,* and *Exodus.*

My classmates sometimes teased me about reading such silly books. How I wanted to tell them that *The Day Lincoln Was Shot, Of Human Bondage,* and *Ethan Frome* were not near as silly as the hot rod and girl stories.

College Years

Later, I was influenced a little more by a young man that I had met. Every time that I would see him, he would always be reading something besides textbooks. He was always anxious to tell me about the stories after he had completed the books. They would always be interesting. At this point I decided to try reading things that were not assigned to me.

I have been slipping my father a book now and then. . . . I'm the only one in my family who has gone on to college and sometimes I feel a bit cut off from them. These books sort of bridge us together. They are a way I share my life with them.

In college there were books everyone was reading. Also if a movie was based on a book, it was important to have read the book so you could point out the differences. I remember books being the center of long discussions in the dorm in which we contemplated the Great Questions of the Universe.

Near the end of my freshman year in college, I began dating a boy whom I had always considered an intellectual superior. Being able to converse with him and to understand many of his ideas and beliefs became quite a challenge. In order to keep up with him I had to start reading again. It wasn't just reading for reading's sake, but reading for knowledge, understanding and insight. All of the summer following my freshman year, I read as though I might never have a chance to do it again.

Adult Years

I was in a London coffee shop when I discovered the loss of my wallet. I couldn't even pay my check. The hostess was very kind and loaned me the money. During our conversation we talked about books and she suggested that I read Oscar Wilde's *De Profundis*. She had just read and enjoyed the book. In fact she had it with her, so I borrowed it. I later bought a copy and have read it twice since.

Most of my friends (during army service in England) were reading two and three books at a time and it began to rub off on me. I have been reading ever since.

I looked forward to teaching, hoping that time would be found then for outside reading, but once again I was disappointed. However, during my second year of teaching some of the younger professional workers in our community organized an informal reading group. We met twice a month for a session which lasted around two hours. This was fun.

During World War II, my husband was overseas for a couple of years and books again became my retreat and sanctuary. This time a group of young adults would meet together for discussion of current books and plays. I got a good smattering of Kathleen Norris, Edna Ferber, Lowell Thomas and *Peyton Place*. Some of these rather disgusted some of us and we started on Shakespeare's works.

When my children were small and my husband and I were of necessity home many evenings, he used to read outloud some of Shakespeare's plays among other things. I saved up ironing and other chores to do as he read. These were very profitable years for us in cementing our marriage.

Reprise

These samples of early reading experiences within the family circle demonstrate the "socializing" quality of books. Here, where concern and affection can be counted upon, the young person learns to interact with parents and siblings. The child who gave her father *The Island of the Blue Dolphins* to read has learned the pleasure generated by sharing and discussing books. The family that all read detective stories was making books a normal social activity instead of a solitary experience.

Family models also greatly influence a young person's attitudes. There are so many accounts of parents who are remembered reading, not just aloud to the child, but alone with their own books. Seeing other members of the family reading made some youngsters curious about what could be so fascinating in the pages of a book. One young person read all the books that the father read as a youth. Another read what a seven-year-older sister was reading and therefore missed all the classics directed at her own age.

Interestingly, books may lay the foundation for many friendships as the young reach elementary school. Books' socializing power often continues throughout the school years and into the adult years as well. In the beginning, such friendships act as a source for appealing reading matter. The children with a wide collection of Nancy Drew or Hardy Boys books attract other individuals with the same interests, and an exchange of books begins. Remember the girl who had an unbelievable collection of the Bobbsey Twins and Sue Barton books? The respondent was instantly attracted to this child. There was another girl, whose best friend had horses, and this mutual interest led to their reading volume after volume of horse and dog stories.

But as young people mature, books may add another dimension in gaining status for these young people with their friends. Often in the high school years, teenagers decide it is time to be more selective in their reading. They seek out current literature and college book lists in order to keep up with others. One boy indicated that he got a "good feeling" when someone mentioned a book that he had read. And that the feeling still persists in adult life. While a senior in high school, one young woman, trying to keep abreast of a boyfriend's reading interests, struggled with Shakespeare, Aeschylus, poets and philosophers, so that she could discuss ideas with him.

During the college and adult years, books become even more important as sources of ideas for discussion with others. Often, the books being read by others act as a challenge to a young adult. Most people need information, and through this information, they gain status or friendship. The young man who lost his wallet in London had a memorable experience, for the hostess not only paid his check, but also loaned him a book that she enjoyed. For him, it became one of the most important books of his life. The exchange between friends of books they have enjoyed is one of the rewarding, continuing experiences for all age groups. It is almost as if we give something valuable of ourselves when we share a book. The discussions that follow mutual readings help individuals expand their own thinking. Thus, books become a tool for social interaction throughout our lives.

7 What Books Do for Readers

Books are assigned many different roles in our society. They are the tools of instruction from elementary school through university graduate programs and in almost every subject-matter field. On a personal level, books may offer individuals a vehicle for escape, aesthetic appreciation, insights into self and the world, and intellectual stimulation. The protocols indicate how varied are the reasons people read books and the effects those books had on the readers' lives.

It is not surprising to find that the reading of books does different things for different people. There are somewhere between twenty-five to fifty behavioral objectives that are claimed to be valid outcomes from the reading of literature. These objectives range from simple enjoyment of a story or poem to knowing the history of humanity's literary endeavor; from becoming an enthusiastic reader to becoming a discriminating reader; from learning how to find books in a library to seeing the intricacies of literary craftsmanship. Of the countless books one reads, what remains in one's mind or memory? Do books change one's thinking or even one's overt behavior? Is reading such a significant activity in one's life that it should be promoted above sports or writing or oral dexterity? Often, the protocols speak to this point. And occasionally they reveal the impact that particular books have made on the respondent.

Books That Create Emotional and Sensory Responses

> I remember that my mother was disturbed by the fact that I believed everything about the stories. I had trouble distinguishing between the real and imaginary worlds. During the day we acted out the stories that we heard at night. I was spanked for some of the play acting like trying to fly like Peter Pan.

> My favorite animal book was *Bambi*, but I always skipped the pages that had the pictures of the forest fire, because they terrified me.

> I remember one book in particular, not because of the story, but

because it was about a white dog with black spots and on every page the spots on the dog were made of material rather than the paper as the rest of the book was. I can still remember how it felt to run my finger over those spots.

The first word that I learned was *look,* and above the word was a picture of Sally putting on her father's golashes. I can even remember that she had on a yellow dress with green sprigs on it.

About the third grade I had just finished a story where a baby had died. I cried and cried. My mother and dad both tried to tell me that it was only a story. I cried myself to sleep not believing them.

Something electric shot through my spinal cord and twanged at my toes, my tummy and my finger tips the first time I read the stories in *Old Favorite Fairy Tales,* my father's gift to me on my eighth Christmas.

One of my favorites was *Little Red Riding Hood.* I had a horrible fascination for the book, because it contained a horrible picture of a vicious wolf hiding behind a tree. I remember studying the picture intently. Needless to say, I developed a terrible fear of wolves and even secretly believed in werewolves.

The next most vivid memory I have is a book called *The Adopted Family.* I and my brothers and sister are adopted and my parents had gotten the book to help us understand. That book really had a profound effect on me. Basically because of it, I feel that I've always known that I was adopted and have always been able to accept it.

Finally the librarian, a stern old woman, recommended *Seatmates.* I read it and loved it. It was a story of a very old fashioned girl who was new to the town. As a new student she had to sit by herself without a seatmate. This book was so important to me that I later reread it in fourth grade and again as an adult.

The first books I recall reading (they were all bound in bright apple-red coverings) were the Great American Series. I picked out only these books to read in the lower grades when library times came around. During this age period I believe I was looking for an identity figure. The book that impressed me most was *Abigail Adams,* because she became so important and yet led such a common childhood. Because the books presented children growing up it was possible to empathize and project myself into the stories. I would frame myself in the portrait of a personable and important lady of the nation.

I read *Black Beauty* seven times and cried harder each time than

I did before. At a tender age I had firmly decided that I would devote my life to caring for old and discarded animals.

Books That Stimulate the Imagination

The one classic which greatly influenced my life was *Robinson Crusoe*. Crusoe and I had much in common. We were both alone on our own little islands — our own little worlds. Crusoe was my idol, so for several months I imagined myself, equipped with a goat skin umbrella and faithful dog, roving over my little island (the back forty on our farm). I still feel a certain affection for *Robinson Crusoe* and make a point of reading the book yearly and recalling the time I first read it.

I remember making a nook for myself in my closet, stealing cold chicken from the kitchen by way of venison, and reading *Robin Hood*. When I grew tired of reading I would run outside and swing wildly from the long vines which grew from the trees which surrounded our house. After reading *Swiss Family Robinson* I built a tree house with my brother.

Nancy Drew books inspired me to write mystery stories in fourth and fifth grades. I often lived my life through Nancy Drew and respected her ability to maneuver herself in dramatic situations. She was everything a girl could want to be: intelligent, attractive, well liked, and an admirable heroine. Her struggles were not necessarily those of puberty but loftier struggles with good and evil.

Heidi was one of my next ventures and I became so intrigued with the goat milk and cheese on which Heidi and her grandfather subsisted that my parents made a special trip to a farm to obtain a sample of goat's milk so that I could decide if it really did have a spicy flavor.

I suppose the books that changed my life more than any others were my father's Horatio Alger books. I thought there was still a chance for success after I read how Ben Worthington and Canfield Whitford overcame their poor backgrounds by hard work and luck.

I read *The Nun's Story* and planned to become a nun. I read *Uncle Tom's Cabin* and became so saintly that my parents were alarmed. I read and reread *Little Women* and took a sudden tomboyish turn.

I placed myself in the position of the female character and indulged myself in feelings of young love or became frustrated when the boy in the story refused to take notice. I think I even employed some of the techniques I had read about for attracting the opposite sex in my own experiences.

And guess what Sherlock Holmes did for me? Though I was fast becoming a mystery fan and reading every passing mystery writer in the library, Sir Conan Doyle did not interest me in the mysterious. I was rather, almost fanatically intrigued with the detective's powers of observation. To this day I catch myself mentally calculating the weight of a shopping bag and its contents from the depth of the heel imprints made in the snow by its carrier.

Salinger's book affected my whole character. I began imitating Holden Caulfield saying "goddam" and labeling everything "phony."

In high school this interest in imaginative and dramatic literature carried me into dramatic arts where one could be a hero and say terribly funny or terribly devastating things to the other characters in the play. It gave me a chance to live another life. It was something I had done with all the characters in all of the books I have ever read. The outcome of this background, this odd manner of dealing with the characters in books, is such that I cannot to this day, keep myself aloof. I tend to identify with the people in the book. These people come alive as I read and I often suffer for days after finishing such a book. As I grow older my enjoyment of books increases and so does the wonder concerning their effect.

I do recall reading *Gone with the Wind* as a junior and reading all 1,300 pages of it practically in one sitting. I remember that I cried bitterly one early, early morning that it had to end at all. I wanted it to go on forever.

Although I enjoy this type of book (*Studs Lonigan, The Cloister and the Hearth, Of Human Bondage*) I feel emotionally drained when I finish one. I become so involved with the characters that I constantly fight feelings of frustration.

The book I remember most is *Cry the Beloved Country* by Alan Paton. I cried all the way through it. Characters varied, but the language was so beautiful.

Books That Trigger New Interests

In the eighth grade, I thought I had found my life's work when we started to study electricity. I even remember trying to read some engineering books, and especially one on armature winding. I read the biography of Thomas Edison and dug into everything I could find on electricity. That was the first year I asked for books for Christmas.

By my last two years my reading tastes had changed to mysteries and war. Strangely enough the war novels were usually documentary. I would spend hours following the blow by blow account of the fall of the Remagen Bridge. I mapped out troop movements of the Battle of the Bulge and of Rommel's Africa corps. Here for once a major impact had been made upon me by literature. Largely through my reading, I decided to major in history in college.

I think Madame Curie became my idol as a result of her biography. At the time I was very interested in science and thought I would one day become a doctor. Her biography was an appealing example. *Arrowsmith* was also about a scientist and therefore another of my favorites. (Hope I have the title right.)

A very definite influence on my reading at this time was a growing interest in science. In the 10th grade I decided medicine was my field and I would become a great woman doctor. Of course, I read Elizabeth Blackwell over and over. Another favorite was *Microbe Hunters*. One of my other favorites was *Madame Curie*, a book I still enjoy. My burning desire to become a doctor faded during my junior year when my progress was blocked by a monster known as Chemistry, but my interest in scientific books remains with me, perhaps because I married a doctor.

I read Frank Slaughter's *Daybreak,* and after reading it, I became interested in the conditions in mental hospitals. I read some more about them including information on New York's Bellevue Hospital. At this time I was considering a major in psychiatry.

Books That Give Solace

As a kid I was clumsy, not over adept at games, a slow runner at best, and did not care too much for the chiding of other kids. So it became increasingly easy for me to choose the reality of books' plots and uncritical characters over the reality of my friends.

In junior high I did not particularly like myself and I was very much a loner. I read a great deal of fantasy and romantic love stories. I especially liked books in which there was a plain, shy girl who blossomed into beauty, inherited great wealth, and became the type of personality that made everyone want to be a close friend of hers.

Books were a haven. They didn't hurt my feelings. If I didn't like a book, I could stop reading whereas situations with flesh and blood people are sometimes hard to control.

I had few friends. I was fat and shy and clumsy. I was not at ease with my peers. Books offered me a place where I felt confident, where I controlled the situation — at least in fantasy — where I could experience so much.

My seventh grade teacher called me an ugly duckling and all the students called me "Brownie." With books I could fantasize and be popular.

Books to me in junior high were a way to escape the adjustment problems of eighth grade and to gain maturity for senior high school. They were my source of information for all the questions I couldn't put into words. They were like having an older brother or sister to show you what was going on and what was to come.

When my mother was dying, I found myself reading *Robinson Crusoe* to my younger brother when there seemed to be nothing left to talk about.

I grew up in an ethnic ghetto in Chicago. One of the reasons I was able to survive my childhood was to get lost in books.

When I was ten my mother died after a long illness and during the weeks before her death, life was anything but normal for us. The afternoon after the funeral I went straight to the library, perhaps as an escape from the house and its depression, but more likely as an attempt to reestablish a familiar pattern and security not present in the weeks of chaos.

Books That Spark New Directions

I escaped from a good part of puberty by burying myself in books. As my peers developed social graces, I was developing a form of literary criticism. I thought of myself as a connoisseur of books, learning to recognize the favorite plots of authors. It gave me roles to play in interaction with my peers.

I have always been reticent and have found it difficult to make friends. Books became my friends. Through reading I could learn things and have friendships which were more interesting than those available to me in a small Arkansas rural community.

Reading was a form of escape, but it was also a cautious route into the real world, where I really wanted to be, but felt nervous about. I wanted lots of maps and instructions and reading provided them.

I remember being terribly crushed about a broken romance and finding my salvation in Erich Fromm and *The Art of Loving*. It was his words that had the greatest impact on my life and its direction.

I began doing poorly in school and finally quit in the second semester of my freshman year in high school. I went back to school the following year but could find no meaning in anything so I quit again. I felt lonely and alienated and grossly different from the kids my age. It was at this time that I read the first book I'd opened in a long time — *The Catcher in the Rye*. I felt after reading it that I wasn't alone in my feelings. Then I read *The Heart is a Lonely Hunter*. One thing led to another, and I eventually decided to go back to school.

But I do know that when I can't stand this old pressured world another minute, there are books on that shelf that can bring me solace and relief. Jesse Stuart's *My Year of Rebirth* was a life saver to us when my own husband had a coronary last Easter. We've given six copies of it to others. Always there is Thomas Wolfe telling me when I want to quit and start over, that "you can't go home again" and that if you ever try, you'll be disappointed because things will not be the same. They change as you change, and that is a life fact that must be accepted. In time of grief there is Edna St. Vincent Millay telling me that the dead must be allowed to bury themselves, cruel as it sounds.

The first book that really made a lasting impression on me was *Door in the Wall* by Marguerite De Angeli. I came into contact with this book in about fifth grade, at the time we were learning about prejudice and discrimination. I loved the story then and still do, mainly because it shows how one can overcome a handicap with a little encouragement.

But Dickens was there, too. I suffered with *David Copperfield*. I marveled at the cruelty of human beings. I winced at the unfairness of life. Somehow I waded through many of these little red leather books, and while they were very serious for a sensitive child, they were probably my greatest insight into human nature, both good and bad.

Stone's *The President's Lady* not long after that helped me to intensify the feeling that something existed in writing which I had been missing for these many years. From that time on I felt that I had begun to read as if for the first time. This was not the end of my growth, to be sure, but rather the beginning. It was some time before I was able to bring any real critical thinking to what I read.

The one book which hit me like a bomb during that period (16 years old) was *Death Be Not Proud*. It was written by John Gunther, and concerns his fifteen-year-old son, who died of an incurable brain tumor. The boy was precocious, inquisitive, lively, and possessed a true reverence for knowledge. He was spirited and kind and honest and sincere. I could not accept his death and would not reconcile it. The fact that this story was a true documentary would not let me pass it off lightly. I was depressed and stunned by that book, and could not get it off my mind. After this book I became obsessed with death. The earth's one incurable neurosis began plaguing me. I was honestly so involved with the philosophical problem of reconciling the death of that boy with my concept of kind nature that I could not concentrate properly on anything else. I believe that this book marked the beginning of my maturer insight into the dilemma of man in the universe.

Eliot exemplified the poet of social commentary which I admired and his *Waste Land* set a new goal for me to work towards in my level of understanding language. He was the perfect writer for this period in my life (high school) — more realistic than Shelley, yet not as raw as Ferlinghetti.

When I read *Of Human Bondage* and *The Razor's Edge* as a senior in high school, they shook my own philosophy right down to the roots. It was not until my junior year in college that I ever got back on really solid ground. I am glad now that something stirred me to enough confusion to get out of my taken-for-granted beliefs and made me seek more information.

In Korea I read everything I could get my hands on from cigarette wrappers to *Catcher in the Rye*, which I picked up in some compartment below decks. Of all the books I read in that three weeks, this was the one that made the deepest impression on me. It was part of a world I had never dreamed existed, a world that drew the monotony, and the fear, and the uncertainty I had previously experienced, and was still experiencing, into focus.

Many of the books I reread, because I can react to them on so many different levels: spiritually, psychologically and symbolically. Books such as *The Invisible Man, House Made of Dawn,* and *Light in August* provide new insight each time I read them.

Reprise

Very young readers are sometimes so affected by a book that the line between the real and the imaginary becomes blurred; a person becomes so engrossed in the reading material that the characters seem to come alive, leaving an intense emotional impact on the reader. Sometimes one remembers a feeling of terror or the tears shed over a sad story such as *Black Beauty.* One young woman could remember the texture of a dog's spots that were made out of cloth, and another recalled the color of Sally's dress on the page where she initially realized that the letters "l-o-o-k" were a word. The memories, all of which are vivid and yet as unlike as one snowflake from another, emphasize the emotional and sensory intensity of certain readers' experiences with books.

The respondents also had vivid memories of books filling their personal needs. One mentioned learning to accept his being an adopted child; another recalled adjusting to a new school. Some identified so closely with the characters in their reading that they acted out *Robinson Crusoe*, for example, or insisted on testing goat's milk for spiciness. There were those who identified so closely with the characters in a story that they felt these characters were really their friends.

The books they read often led some of the respondents to attempt to imitate fictional creations. One young woman mentioned using the same techniques as those of Janet Lambert's characters for attracting the opposite sex; another reader changed her own personality to match that of the heroine in the current novel she was reading.

Perhaps one of the most important findings was the impact of *Catcher in the Rye* on its readers. The reactions varied from the young man who adopted Holden Caulfield's favorite expletives, to those respondents who found comfort in Holden's confusion and bitterness because they mirrored the readers' own feelings.

It was not surprising to find that many participants in this study remembered books as a way of escaping from the reality of their own lives. For some, books provided a fantasy life that seemed better than their own. Others used books for solace and security in times of family death, as did one respondent who, as the family's mother lay dying, read *Robinson Crusoe* to a little brother. One young woman, crushed by a broken love affair, found comfort and direction from reading *The Art of Loving*. A somewhat older respondent called Jesse Stuart's *My Year of Rebirth* a lifesaver after her own husband had a heart attack. Thus, books offer new vistas and ideas that are intimately shared by the reader.

Most interesting is the discovery that a certain group of books seems to merit the label "watershed" books. These books create a dividing line in the reader's thinking and may be responsible for redirecting one's life. In most of the protocols, there was generally one book that stood out in memory because of its vividness and impact. *Death Be Not Proud, The Adopted Family, The Art of Loving,* and *Of Human Bondage* are a few mentioned in this chapter. Others that were cited often in the autobiographies but are not mentioned here include *Walden,* which led one respondent to value simplicity; *Stranger in a Strange Land,* for the ethical questions it proposed; and *Demian* for the search for self that it generated in the respondent. *Catcher in the Rye* was without doubt the book most frequently mentioned as a milestone by the male respondents. Not every reader remembers a "watershed" book, but for those who do, there are different ones to serve people in different ways. Although these books appear at no predictable period in an individual's life, their impact is never forgotten.

Interestingly, whatever the reason for a book's appeal, seldom was the respondent's memory of the book consciously associated with the book's degree of literary merit. More often than not, what the writer remembered was the emotional impact of the book, the insights it provided whether for self or others, and the growth that it stimulated in the reader. The writers of the autobiographies described books as kindling the imagination, creating visions of life's possibilities, giving expression to the reader's own inarticulate feelings, as well as affecting their emotions, intellectual pursuits, and attitudes. In this way, books provide readers with a continuing, evolving view of both themselves and the world.

8 Subliterature

We are concerned, here, with two kinds of reading material that can be grouped together under the umbrella category of "subliterature": the first is so designated because, although it has the attributes of literature — plot, character, setting, and climax — it is created according to set formulas that have predictable appeal to a certain body of readers. This type of reading material may contain adventure, swift violence, slapstick humor, and impossible romances. Included in this group are innocuous materials such as comics, juvenile series books, sentimental romances, and exotic adventure stories. Periodically, there are outcries against the reading of such material by young people. Until recently, libraries refused to place comics or series books on their shelves because this material did not measure up to approved literary standards. More recently, educators have protested the sexual and ethnic stereotyping presented in series books. Others attack the literary style of series books as pernicious to the development of literary taste in young people.

Our respondents revealed a second type of book and magazine that they read on the sly, partially because this type of reading material was considered "hot stuff." In this second group, some of the adult books are actually of high literary quality but contain profanity and portray explicit sexual activity: for example, *Catcher in the Rye*, *The Grapes of Wrath*, and *Lady Chatterley's Lover*. These titles and others like them fall into the category we have termed "taboo reading." We are not interested in the exact titles as much as in showing that the reading of such material is a normal stage of development. In recent years, even the authors and publishers of teenage books have recognized adolescents' interest in their growing sexuality, and books such as Blume's *Forever*, which deals with teenage sexuality, are found now even in some elementary school libraries. However, self-appointed guardians of public morals have mounted successful campaigns to ban these books in individual communities, probably making them all the more attractive to young readers.

It is important for teachers and parents to realize that both types of subliterature described here serve a purpose in the reading growth

87

of young people. In fact, the majority of the respondents indicated the importance that such material had in "hooking" them on reading. Following are typical comments that are roughly organized around the following types: comics, juvenile series, sentimental romances, and books read on the sly.

Comics

I clearly remember my single handed toppling of a large rotating comic book rack at Paul Farley's Super Value in Des Moines. As a five year old, I regularly spent an hour sprawled on the floor next to that rack reading Superman and Marvel Group comics while my parents did the Saturday shopping.

I guess I turned to the local drug stores rather than fight this woman (librarian) because I had become an avid comic book reader. I can remember holing up with some neighbors in a secluded corner and together with a king size box of crackers, we'd devour both them and Captain Marvel or Plastic Man for hours on end.

Speaking of comic books, I think the reason I wanted to learn to read was so that I could read the comics in the daily paper.

The only kind of reading I might have done that my mother disapproved of was romance comics. She would not let me buy them. I remember sneaking two of my friend's into the house and hiding them in my bedroom closet.

I indulged in the usual childhood fascination for comics. Comics were a local institution on our block and it was something of an adventure to take a stack of comics out and trade them with my neighbors. My interest in comics ran the gauntlet of interests from Bugs Bunny, Donald Duck, Captain Marvel, Superman, westerns, war comics and some romances at a later stage.

Sometime around third grade, perhaps fourth, I discovered comics, much to the chagrin of my parents. For a number of years their effect on my outlook was profound, and not altogether bad. Comics, predominantly Marvel, Hulk, Fantastic Four, Spiderman, etc. enlarged my vocabulary and challenged my imagination.

The comic book was almost non-existent for me. My Mother didn't believe in them. My girl friends' rooms with their stacks and stacks of comic books seemed like heaven to me. Once in awhile Mom would break down and buy me a Buzzy or Date with Judy comic.

I remember that trading and saving comic books was a major business enterprise about the fourth and fifth grades and my brother and I had a collection of upwards of 250 to 300 comic books of all flavors.

Juvenile Series

The libraries in both schools were sadly inadequate, and therefore I read nearly everything available and many books I read two and three times each, simply because there was nothing else. I went through the Bobbsey Twins series, the Mother West Wind series and all the Horatio Alger books.

I read the Joe Strang series and hundreds of funny books and cartoon stories. These cartoon stories came in hard covers but were designed for little hands. They were about an inch and a half thick and two or three inches square. They cost ten cents each. Some of them were about flying aces in the First World War and were true stories. When my dimes ran out, as they constantly did, I swapped books with other kids. At times I had as high as sixty of these books on hand. I never kept them for the sake of keeping them, except for the histories of flying aces, but read as many of them as I could and ran to trade for more. Sometimes I read ten or twelve of them in one night.

Our tiny drugstore got in a supply of Horatio Alger at fifteen cents each; my ambition was to own the complete series. During a siege of measles, I bullied my family into buying me six.

Nancy Drew became my friend. I shared every adventure she had and helped solve the mysteries. I think the Nancy Drew series led me to think in terms of being a writer myself. I spent hours and hours writing novels with myself playing the role of Nancy.

The first book I bought all by myself was a Nancy Drew book. I remember looking at the better things on the shelf, but temptation was too great and I came out with *The Sign of the Twisted Candles*.

I guess I read everything I could get my hands on, particularly anything that was exciting or adventurous. I remember reading a lot of Tom Swift and Tarzan novels. We had a fairly large set of books at home. My mother was and is a great reader. I can remember many times when I wouldn't know the meanings of words and I would ask her. She always knew. I also used to read the dictionary and encyclopedia. Still do, once in a while.

The same year (eighth grade) we had a book burning in my grade school. One nun had caught one of the eighth grade girls reading a Gidget book. It had been passed around the class so everyone could read the "dirty" parts. Right before it was due to come to me the nun got hold of it. Being a good Catholic school we were all strongly admonished and the book was burned.

At that time Penny's and the Five & Ten in our town devoted considerable space at Christmas time to displaying loads of twenty-five cent adventure stories, cheaply bound and printed, but hard bound like real books and these we could and did own. I can still remember some of the titles, some of which I still have, even if I dare not read them again. *Lost in the Wilds of Brazil, Lost on the Moon, The Mystery of Gaither Cove, The Secret of the Armour Room.* My brother and I founded our own book club, read aloud to each other on Friday nights and became sophisticated literary critics.

Sentimental Romances

Grace Livingston Hill was the only author whose books I would read. I was a Sunday school girl, and I suppose that I liked these, because the plots had the theme of people not knowing God and Jesus Christ. The times I could find none of her books, I would settle for books that were shelved in the neighborhood of Hill's books.

"Put that book down and get to bed or there will be no book tomorrow!" It wasn't that mother did not want me to read, of course: this was a routine matter of health and discipline. The book was *The Shepherd of the Hills* and I could not tear myself from it. How it came into a country preacher's bookcase I don't know — the point is that *it was there,* so I read it. So was *Ishmael* there. My college brother came home and asked me why I was reading that junk. I didn't know any reading was junk. Because it was there and because it transported me from a humdrum world to an exciting world, it was good.

The Girl of the Limberlost destroyed my apathy. My backyard creek became the dangerous swamp. Cabbage moths took on the glory of the breath taking Luna moth. One "no" from my mother would transform her momentarily into the hard, uncomprehending Mrs. Comstock. And I palpitated harmoniously with Elnora as she experienced love.

The Shepherd of the Hills thrilled me to the point of reading the whole book in one day, a record at that time (Jr. high).

I remember that I worked in the Junior high library and sneaked out Grace Livingston Hill novels in my book satchel. I hid them under my pillow at home and read them late at night when I should have been sleeping. It was very important that no one catch me reading these love stories. I was a year younger than my peers, having skipped the second grade, and consequently lagged behind them in my development. I had become very proud of my reputation as a scorner of adolescent lust, and to have everyone know that I too was subject to physical and psychological change would have been indeed humiliating.

My teen time reading of westerns seems to have filled two needs in my life: something to do that did not cost anything but time and a city boy's longing for the outdoor world and the escape it seemed to provide for a poverty-sore lad walled in by a large city in which he felt helpless to do anything about any of his hungers.

I had the covers from an old Latin book which I constantly refilled with novels to read in class. I flunked Latin, but I saved hundreds of hours which would have been wasted otherwise. These novels were Zane Grey types and adventure stories. Really, I didn't select them but just read anything that I could get my hands on. There were sweetness and light novels of the 1890s and mountains of magazines and a few big city gangster stories.

Sometimes in the middle of the night I would read the books my mother had pushed to the back of the bookcase because she thought they were too immoral.

Books Read on the Sly

When my mother learned that I had innocently exchanged our magazines for some entitled *True Confessions* and *True Story,* she very promptly returned those issues to the neighbor with no comment to me other than, "Those stories are not the type for you to read." It was not until some years later that I realized what the *True Confessions* magazines really were.

A neighbor girl moved away and donated her entire collection of *True Story* and *True Romance* magazines to me. There were piles of them. For weeks I supplied myself nightly with apples and popcorn and, pop-eyed with revelation, devoured bushels and pans and pages. On the night that I turned the final page, I completed my lifetime's reading of true confession publications.

I even read the confession type magazines that my mother kept for some unknown reason. Those magazines provided some very traumatic experiences, not only because I knew Mother and Father condemned them strongly, but because the actions of the characters seared my strongly idealistic and naive nature. But I read them from time to time with a fascinated horror.

Sometime along about Junior High I made the acquaintance of a magazine called *Love Story* and I can recall reading this monthly for awhile. I also remember quite clearly that after several months of this I became aware of the fact that each story was just like the other one — that there was a pattern which one could follow without effort and I was bored by this.

I loved to read movie magazines, but had neither the nerve nor the money to buy copies of my own. We had a friend who was a beauty operator, and I used to read while waiting for her to be free to talk to me.

Sometime during this period I discovered the "true" periodicals — *True Story, True Romance* and so on, ad absurdum. During the day they were carefully hidden beneath the mattress. At bedtime I would gloat or cry (most likely the latter) over the "soap opera" type story. This period was very short lived, thanks, not to my discriminating taste, but to my mother's enthusiasm for cleanliness.

Also at this age, I entered the stage of pulp movie and true romance magazines. Secretly at the beauty shop or at a girl friend's home these were digested with relish. Because I was a late maturing girl, these did not become more than a phase of interest — out of curiosity more than anything.

True Story and *True Confessions* were banned by my parents, but I read them at school anyway, until I became bored with them. Movie magazines were a little more tolerated in my home, but I wasn't very interested in them, therefore I didn't read these often. *National Geographic* magazine was my favorite, especially those issues that described a foreign country and their way of living.

When I was sixteen, I went through a period of "dirty books," most of which I would now consider pretty tame. *Candy* was probably the worst.

Seventh graders weren't allowed to check out *Spirit Lake*. Someone stole it and we passed it around.

One vivid memory I have of high school is borrowing *Peyton Place* from one of my friends. I hid it under my pillow and read a little every night.

I can remember Henry Miller's *Sexus* going around study hall in 25 page sections.

I remember a porno book, *Feeling No Pain*. There were about ten of us who read that. I hid it under my mattress at home and read it behind another book. We also read a similar type book aloud at a slumber party.

I became intrigued with "dirty books." I remember my mother's shock at the realization that I was reading such books as *Mandingo* and *Fanny Hill*.

I can remember reading a book called *Millie*, which was not only trash but my first experience with any kind of "sexy" novel. It was the kind of book which is passed from locker to locker when the teacher isn't looking. It concerned, among other things, incest. This did not strike me with the impact that it might have, because although I realized it was naughty, I simply was not aware of such things and felt they were part of a different world.

When I was in fifth or sixth grade, we had a hired man who bought *True Story* and *True Confessions* magazines. I used to skip into his room for an hour or so after school and devour those love stories, sordid and otherwise, until all at once one day, I found I was sick of them and never cared to look at another.

Reprise

The demimonde of literature seems to exist at most stages of the reading pattern. It appeals and thrives from the moment that individuals read and select materials for themselves until they become mature adults. Tastes seem to follow a kind of developmental pattern. At the earlier stages, there is the reading of comic books, and, almost always, comic books rather than comic strips. The enthusiasm for comic books seems to fade into a similar addiction for the juvenile series books, often with the same protagonist in book after book. The pattern is one exciting adventure after another, all built on a few formulas.

A bit later, magazines of the sensational variety come into their own. Supposedly, these magazines are geared to the adult reader, but actually, the teenage reader is the implied audience. At about the same time, the adolescent discovers the more sensational adult best-sellers, especially those with erotic innuendoes. Later, the maturing reader may also discover some of the "real shockers" of the literary world. These volumes may include some of the classics of pornographic literature, such as *Candy* or *Fanny Hill*, or they may be works of stature like *Lady Chatterley's Lover*, which originally reached acclaim through attempted censorship. The demimonde books attract readers at the early stages of their reading development. The books may continue to be appealing throughout adult life, in spite of the attempts of educators, acting on behalf of the socially righteous, to subvert this appeal.

The protocols suggest that this body of literature is read passionately. One writer stated that a desire for learning to read was sparked even by a desire to read comics. Comic books are read avidly in the corner store that stocks them and other such magazines. These books are often the first ones bought for or by a child, and the need to read more brings about the old-fashioned barter system of trading them for different ones. Often, the teenagers become so engrossed that they read all night. In school, readers of these materials sometimes conceal the books behind the covers of school texts so that they can continue reading during the school day.

Adults instill a sense of guilt in young people about reading this so-called subliterature. The protocols revealed mostly clandestine reading of subliterature by young adults. Parents, siblings, librarians, and teachers objected to the reading of such material. A mother banned these books by hiding them behind other volumes on the bookshelves. A nun conducted a book burning. A college-age brother sneeringly called such books "trash." Consequently, teenagers sometimes felt embarrassed and ashamed if they were "caught" reading this material. But in spite of the negative reactions from others, adolescents continue to read subliterature. This makes a strong statement about the futility of adults trying to control the reading selections of young people.

Subliterature is a part of young people's culture. Sometimes they collect these books as they collect stamps or dolls or baseball cards. Lending and trading of books and magazines are commonplace. A few ingeniously set up lending libraries, and later, they surreptitiously pass "hot" books around among their classmates and sometimes read choice passages at slumber parties. The reading of these books and magazines seems almost necessary for membership in a peer group.

Only occasionally is there an indication of the impact of subliterary material upon readers other than in its transitory power to draw them to it. The most obvious attraction is the excitement and adventure that it presents, which is seldom to be found in everyday life. As with other literature, readers empathize with the characters and sometimes imaginatively role play the part of the protagonists they read about. At more mature stages, there is no doubt that some of the material titillates the readers. Sometimes this is a traumatic experience. One young lady says her idealistic nature was "seared by these books." There seems little doubt that subliterature plays a part in the teenager's loss of innocence; the books expose behavior that is unrealistic to the experiences of the young person.

Like gambling, drinking, and prostitution, demimonde literature is always there and will probably always be read. As with other types of literature, it has been a part of all civilizations both past and present, no matter what steps have been taken toward its eradication. As forbidden fruit, it only becomes more attractive for the reader. But there is one important thing that can be said for it. This material, albeit in simplified form, acquaints the young with all the conventions upon which great literature is built: plot, characterization, dialogue, suspense, and irony. Throughout their lives, many adults turn to subliterature not for its literary attributes, but because it provides them with an avenue of escape into an unreal world where life has more of everything: excitement, adventure, love, sex, fear, hate, violence. By living at such a high pitch, even the adult reader can forget, for a few hours, the humdrum routine and problems of everyday life.

9 Teachers and Teaching: The Secondary School Years

In elementary schools, the English language subjects are divided into a number of areas: penmanship, spelling, reading, writing and grammar, and, at times, something called "literature." But beginning at the seventh or eighth grade levels, students encounter a subject labeled "English," which consists largely of literature and composition. English courses could have a major impact on the reading and attitudes of teenagers, but unfortunately, the objectives of literary study in the secondary schools have never really been agreed upon. Should such programs teach young people *about* literature or should they teach *through* literature? Should they emphasize literary *form* or should they emphasize literary *content*? Should they teach *close reading* of a text or should they encourage *wide and extensive reading*? Should they systematically present the major selections of the literary heritage that *all* educated persons might be expected to know, or should they present a smorgasbord of books from which *individual* students could plan an individualized menu for their own consumption of literary works?

Our study participants came from many different kinds of secondary schools; often within the same school, one teacher would present one point of view about what and how literature should be studied, while a second teacher would present an entirely different viewpoint. Therefore, it is not surprising that, between school systems, there were widely divergent objectives for the classroom. You will find a number of common reactions in the protocols about favorable and unfavorable English classes. We have included only a few references to the classics in this chapter; reactions to them were so numerous that they are discussed in a separate chapter.

Teachers

> The one book I remember most (junior high) is Irene Hunt's *Up a Road Slowly*. It was recommended to me by my English teacher and I remember that at the time she made me feel as though she

had thought about it and decided this was the best book for me to read. It has remained special to me.

I would have maintained a diet of teenage romances if it hadn't been for an English teacher in junior high. She gave us a reading wheel, a drawing of a wheel with spokes indicating different types of reading — science fiction, biography, poetry, etc. — to fill in during the school year. I was determined to fill in every blank spot on the paper. It meant reading in fields I had never touched before.

I think eighth grade must have been a turning point in my life as far as books were concerned. I had a teacher whom I liked and admired very much. She seemed to take a very personal interest in my reading habits and she did much to change them for the better, I think. It was during this time that I read several of Elizabeth Goudge's books and enjoyed them very much. This same teacher during my early high school years kept me interested in such authors as Daphne Du Maurier and Evelyn Waugh.

In junior high the importance of reading quantities of literature was so constantly pounded into my head by all my English teachers that I began worrying a great deal about not doing enough reading. I had such difficulty finding reading time (I spent many hours daily on homework from seventh grade on) and I was supposed to read so much. It was a great frustration for me and may have caused me to read less simply because I felt I couldn't keep up. That I wasn't reading enough was a dark cloud always hovering over my head.

In the seventh grade, I had an English teacher who never ceased to berate me for my bad spelling and my ineptitude for English grammar. She once stood me up and made me repeat definitions for what seemed like the whole period. I was terrified. I had always found it hard to explain anything except with the aid of a diagram, and I hated nothing quite so much as oral recitation. After seventh grade, the mere mention of English, language or literature, made me break out in a cold sweat, and I am sorry to say that I never enjoyed another English class or anything I associated with it until my freshman year in college.

My seventh grade teacher decided that I was reading too much fiction and assigned me to read a book about the Antarctic or some other such place (I remember penguins). This wouldn't have been so bad except she suspended my Bookmobile privileges until I finished it. It took me six months to read that book and I hated every second of it.

I remember reading *The Pearl* as a freshman and my teacher discussed the book with his Cliffs Notes in hand. Needless to say I didn't get much out of it. I felt offended, I think, that Mr. G. needed notes in order to lead a discussion.

My ninth grade English teacher was a sweet, gentle lady who loved all of us dearly but who was convinced that she was failing us if she didn't induce us to love Sir Walter Scott. So I fled from the thickets of medieval mysteries to Sherlock Holmes.

In high school, I believe, I really started to read and buy books on my own. However, I feel that the reason for this was the high caliber of English Literature and Language teachers under whom I studied. They made all of the books and writings that we studied sort of "come alive" and this encouraged us to go out on our own. I became very interested in the writings of the twenties and thirties. The books of Sinclair Lewis were especially interesting to me.

The second important event in developing my taste for good books was my sophomore year in high school. My English teacher, Mr. R., handed out two reading lists. One list contained books primarily for adolescents; the other listed the author and title of famous classics. First, I read a few of the adolescent books. Then, I started reading the classics and gradually abandoned reading books written especially for young people. My English teacher required a certain number of book reports, but he also encouraged the students to read more books required. With his encouragement I read 34 books that semester — the greatest number in the class. Consequently I felt very proud, especially after I received a good grade in English.

When I entered high school, it was my good fortune to have an English teacher who guided my desire to read more. Through the ninth grade and into the tenth, I had read very few books outside the class of adolescent reading. In the tenth grade, however, this teacher led me to books far outside the adolescent reading. I began reading the great books, sometimes enjoying them and sometimes not. One that I did enjoy but did not fully understand was *Wuthering Heights*.

In high school, I joined a club called *Literati* and remember reading "good books." This group was sponsored by one of those dedicated teachers who really hope to open new horizons to pupils. For the first time, I realized that there were books of a caliber that was above the general run; that there was such a thing as "good" literature; that there was a difference in style, in message, in values.

We had small group discussions made up of individuals who had certain readings in common. We shared our opinions and interpretations, our likes and dislikes. We each maintained a Reader's Diary in which we recorded our own impressions of the works including favorite quotes and what the book meant to us personally.

In eleventh grade, our teacher of American heritage, a thwarted actor, really made the material come alive. I remember dramatizing *Our Town*, reading aloud "The Tell-Tale Heart" and retelling short stories which each of us prepared individually. I remember being bored by William Bradford's diary and laughing hysterically at Thoreau's account of catching a pig.

I loved all the literature classes in high school and in my senior year we had a memorable class in Shakespeare given by one of those rare persons who could transmit her love of Shakespeare to her class — to me at least. She read, we read, and then we dramatized, both at school and at home on our own. We used to dramatize poems on our own, too (although this was before high school) without any teacher help.

My senior English teacher really opened the door to reading for me. We were introduced to contemporary novelists as well as the classics. Our teacher gave us reading lists and encouraged us to come in and discuss books with him.

I had a wonderful English teacher my senior year in high school. He was the one who introduced us to current literature and the school of realism. We learned about *Main Street* then. I began to read adult fiction and historical novels, especially those written by Scott.

My senior English teacher took an interest in my work. The modular scheduling at Evanston gave the teachers flexibility so that they had time to talk with students. In this way I had many good discussions with Mr. S. We discussed books we had both read, and he recommended books for further reading. He encouraged exploration of my personal interests and gave me credit for this type of independent study.

Teaching Methods

We had an English teacher that several times a month would give us a whole period to read anything we wanted. That I really enjoyed, and no hour ever passed more quickly than that one did. I could never believe it when the bell rang, and it was time to go to the next class.

I also began to read more frequently when I took a course in twelfth grade called Individualized Reading. The course was graded entirely on the amount of books you read. At that time I liked politics and read stories about negative utopias. I read *Brave New World*, *1984*, *Animal Farm*, and *Convention*. My teacher thought I was getting too bogged down with political books and so recommended J. D. Salinger and William Golding. I feel this course introduced me to literature and influenced me toward majoring in English.

Another class my senior year was the Individualized Reading course. The object was for the student to read and briefly report on books chosen from a list. This course was designed to give the brighter student fair credit for his reading prowess. We were encouraged to read at our own pace and glean what we could from each novel. Unfairly the greater number of books reported on, the higher the grade.

In high school with the exception of one teacher, we had an almost entirely free reading program. The only unfortunate thing was that most of the reports were written which took some of the pleasure from reading. My teachers let me choose my own books with an occasional suggestion. I usually tried the books they suggested and found most of them fascinating reading experiences.

At about fifteen my reading matter consisted of Zane Grey and more Zane Grey. I read every book I could find of his and even resorted to other western novels if his were not available. My craze was abruptly brought to an end one day when my tenth grade English teacher informed me I was reading utter trash and that I should not waste my time with such filth. I believe I was so embarrassed in front of my classmates that even today I can't think of Zane Grey without recalling my embarrassment.

In high school my reading experience was anything but happy. There was no freedom of choice. We were asked to read a particular book. Although I did not find the book entertaining, the teacher told me the book was good, but she never explained why or what was good about the book. I wondered why one book was better than another — or why another book was considered a classic and the next one was not. The teachers — all three high school English teachers — failed to satisfy me as to why I should read a certain book. To aggravate matters, the writing of the book report inevitably followed the reading of the book. Invariably the reports had to include a biographical sketch of the author, the period, the setting, the listing of the major and minor characters, a summary of the plot, and finally (which was considered the most important part of the report) what I learned or got from the book. Bewilderment led to resentment. I wasn't reading anything for sheer entertainment as I once had. When I finished high school there lingered a sense of guilt of not having read enough.

Silas Marner came along with sophomore English. I did enjoy it except for the extra work of writing a chapter of our own. If there is a person today who cannot recite Mark Antony's funeral oration, then he didn't take Sophomore English as I knew it. From Junior English the only thing I remember is the teacher's wearing the same three dresses all year long.

The most shattering discovery of my reading life was made by

Silas Marner when we studied it in tenth grade. The slow pace was deadening, but doubly so because I read the whole story while we were still discussing the first part. The worst part of the experience was the *Silas Marner* notebook which was monumental, and which I was sure would give me an "A," but which I unfortunately lost the day it was due and had to do it all over. The second time through was ghastly. *Julius Caesar* was not much more harmonious. The more lines one memorized, the more extra credit he was given. The experience of writing as many lines as possible compared in unpleasantness to playing a solo in a solo contest.

She stretched the study of *Silas Marner* to a full semester's activity. We made notebooks having to scour magazines for pictures illustrating events in the tale, six pictures per chapter. We were graded on how neatly the pictures were pasted on paper, how well our captions were centered on the page. I still have the notebook: I can't bring myself to burn that monument to busy work.

I can recall a very enlightening experience in high school. I admired my sophomore English teacher, because he was well versed in literature and was an actor. One of the most rewarding experiences I had in regard to literature was when this teacher had the class read *Romeo and Juliet* and *West Side Story* simultaneously and compare the two plays. He wanted the students to compare a play by Shakespeare with a modern play so that they would accept the relevance of Shakespeare.

I don't remember disliking immensely any required reading in high school with the exception of *David Copperfield* and *Silas Marner.* Both were good to read once, but we spent weeks on each one. I cringe at the thought of how much time was spent going over these works, word by word and paragraph by paragraph.

Then in tenth grade I discovered Mark Twain. I enjoyed these books a great deal until my English teacher tried to change my reading habits. She thought that *Jane Eyre* would be just the book for me. I didn't like the English teacher and I didn't like the book and there my reading stopped. Except for required assignments I stopped reading altogether until the end of my freshman year in college.

Every English teacher handed out a long list of the classics that every college bound student should read. From then on, my reading appetite was inhibited, because I felt guilty reading anything else and didn't have enough background or support from the teacher to enjoy the classics. I only read because I thought I needed the basic background and I rarely had enough motivation to finish a book.

My high school teacher, for a test, made us memorize nit picky things from Chaucer so the thing I remember from that class is that one pilgrim rode a dapple gray horse named Scot and one had carbuncles on his face.

Most of the books I enjoyed until we analyzed them to death in class. I also hated writing papers to see how close I could come to describing the teacher's opinion of the books, since it seemed that's how they were graded.

I hated having to analyze in high school and in my core literature course because the specific nature of the style didn't matter to me. I didn't read a book, because it was written perfectly but because its content appealed to me. Nor do I very often consciously accept or reject the "statement" a book has to offer. It is very internal and private with me.

One of the most influencing factors that "turned me off" of classroom reading and discussion was the fact that three fourths of my instructors had their set interpretation of the author's message and they, of course, were always right. I don't know how many times I would offer my viewpoint and be told I was wrong with no explanation as to why.

In high school, I think I started to develop my first real distaste of literature. The teachers, as I recall, never really let us have our own interpretation. I disliked most poetry, *Julius Caesar,* and hated Chaucer.

When I was a ninth grader, our English teacher assigned book reports as extra credit work. She handed out a reading list and we were to select from these books which were on reserve at the public library. During that entire year I never failed to read at least one book per week. This was a glorious time for me as I could read as much as time would permit and also I had my first opportunity to use the library.

My freshman year in high school brought about a much closer association with my classmates and teachers. *The Rime of the Ancient Mariner* was read in English class which I thoroughly enjoyed. We were still required to make those confounded book reports, but now we were allowed to choose books for ourselves instead of selecting from a list. I began reading various types of fiction.

In tenth grade, our book report outline was modified somewhat so that we were no longer required to summarize the book "blow by blow," but rather to record twenty new-learned facts. This, to me, gave a more practical reason for reading, and I found the act of reading more enjoyable.

In tenth grade we did interesting things with book reports. We

acted books out in full costume. We read books and then served
as interviewer or reporter with one another, asking questions about
the books. At the end of the year the class divided into groups
of five and each group presented a novel panel, three days in
length on a particular book.

I did not seem to have much time (junior high) to read for
enjoyment anymore, because there was so much required reading
as well as many extra curricular activities. I learned how to fake
book reports. In high school, there was even less time. Here I
also discovered Cliffs Notes and rather than use them as a guide,
I depended on them. Soon I began to hate doing any required
reading and as much as I could — I didn't. Surprisingly I was on
the honor roll, an honors English student.

Sometime in school I had to start writing book reports. They were
terrible, but I learned that Classic Comics were a big help.

Although I enjoyed reading in school I hated to write book reports.
One time my Mother made me stay in after school until I had
read *Kidnapped* and had written a report on it. I haven't read any
Stevenson since.

Most of the books were read or assigned book reports in school.
When reading a book under such conditions, I found it was hard
to obtain real enjoyment from the story since I was more concerned
with the specific details including setting, time, place, and description of the characters.

Book reports in a sense destroyed the enjoyment I derived from
reading. I loved to read just for the sake of reading and learning
something new. But reading came to mean remembering insig-
nificant details in order to make a book report — reading in order
to get a grade and to fulfill a requirement.

I remember being caught short for a book report one day. I had
seen the movie *Lost Horizon* and had liked it very much, and
knowing that we had the book at home, I decided to make a
report on it. Miss E., the teacher, was not fooled, though I did
my best to assure her that I had read the book. Later, I felt very
guilty about the whole matter, and that evening I went home and
started to read the book. I don't remember if I ever finished it,
but from that time on, I started to skim most of the books I chose
to read for the rest of the year's quota.

I suppose the taste for adventure in general prevailed into eighth
grade and my first year of high school where the James Fenimore
Cooper type literature held sway. Simultaneously, however, we
were in the throes of our first exposure to the classics, and they
just weren't reaching me. Praise be to Classic Comics. Were it not
for these ready-made, vivid and complete summaries, no book
report of mine (and a good many other peoples) would ever have

crossed a teacher's desk. Perhaps it wasn't so much a genuine dislike of classical literature as it was an unwillingness to be distracted from my preoccupation with sports and social involvements.

I can remember giving an oral book report on *The Old Man and the Sea* which was a great success, so I proceeded to give the same report for the next two years.

In the high school in the nearby town to which I transferred at the beginning of grade nine, the library consisted of relatively few books of fiction and biography, as well as a few reference books. I think that the library was used only to secure books which one needed for book reports. There were only two of these required each year, but what torment! Book reports were oral, and if you consider yourself to be a "country hick," it is dreadfully frightening to appear in front of a class. Two books which I remember reading for reports and which impressed me were *Up From Slavery* and *Madame Curie* written by her daughter.

During my high school days we were required to make detailed book reports in all of our English classes which in a way dampened my enthusiasm for reading, because I didn't like remembering all of the necessary details after enjoying a book. However, since it was one way to earn extra credit, I would reluctantly write the book report in order to receive a better grade.

Reprise

In secondary school, English becomes a discipline within the curriculum. This coincides with the beginning of complaints that required reading takes up all the student's time and with the decline in pleasure reading. In many of the protocols, required reading is not equated with pleasure. The quantity and kind of selections as well as the methods by which they are taught are a source of criticism. The positive recollections, both in junior and senior high school, are associated with an enthusiastic teacher and some degree of freedom in selection.

You may recall that, in a preceding chapter, the protocols focused on the teacher's reading aloud. In this section, we have included a few representative examples of the positive effects of this practice. One writer described the drama coach who made Shakespeare's works interesting. Other references to success with Shakespeare, not included here, frequently mention the teacher reading the various acts and scenes aloud. Another person, included here, remembered a young high school teacher reading poetry and mythology to the class.

One of the respondents makes a good point about high school teachers guiding the reading interests of students. Here, a successful teacher is reported as giving students two lists: the first presented books written for adolescents and the other presented authors and titles recommended for adults. Built into that exercise is the psychology of freedom of choice, an aspect that makes requirements palatable. Other writers had positive recollections of dramatizing literature. Making literature visual not only gives students a change of pace, but also adds a dimension that seemingly brings literature alive, making it memorable. Another writer mentioned being in a small discussion group that shared opinions and interpretations on certain common readings. This group also recorded in a "Reader's Diary" their favorite quotes, little notes on their reactions, and explanations of what the book meant to them personally. There were also a number of respondents who spoke positively about their experience with individualized reading courses. Here, again, the attraction is greater freedom of choice as opposed to regimented requirements. There were also other comments about particular courses that students found exciting. In general, these reports suggested that having a mixture of modern and classic books makes the offerings more enjoyable.

Complaints were offered about the methods by which required reading is taught. The most frequent criticisms were that the length of time was boringly long and that the analysis of details killed the enjoyment. Another complaint centered on the teacher's asking students to voice their opinions about what a story meant. When they did this, the students perceived that their ideas were wrong unless they matched those of the teacher. These comments may be valid observations; yet they might also spring from the old-fashioned myth that a teacher, like the Delphi oracle, knew and spoke the absolute truth.

As a teaching tool for reading literature, book reports came under heavy fire. Those protocols with positive reactions were based, again, on a sense of freedom of choice. For one respondent, receiving extra credit made the assignment palatable. For another, the lack of a set reading list helped. Alternative methods such as acting out books or presenting books by panels seem favorably received. The major objection was directed at the form requirements of the report: biographical author sketch, the historical period, the setting, description of major characters, summary of the plot, meaning of the author or what was learned from reading the book. The multitude of details that were demanded killed enjoyment for many students. The requirements were seen as a drudgery that could have been helped by a flight to Cliffs Notes or Classic Comics.

Perhaps the best atmosphere for the study of literature during the secondary years is one in which the individuals have a vehicle for sharing personal responses. As it is now used, the book report is often too restrictive. Study of a literary work should be neither too extended nor too belabored with details. Required readings should include both modern and classic works. Discussions should permit a variety of interpretations. And above all, such an atmosphere should include, to the greatest degree possible, opportunities for freedom of choice in selecting literary works.

10 Libraries and Librarians

In a previous chapter we looked at what the protocols revealed about sources for books — those discovered by accident and those coming from family or friends. Any discussion of sources must include the library. Because most of the respondents, in general, have been lifelong users of libraries, we thought it important that this institution receive special attention.

What follows are the respondents' memories of both school and public libraries and the librarians who worked there. You will notice the vivid recollections of early experiences that, in many cases, engendered a permanent attitude. You will hear what the writers have to say about rules and regulations, the ambience, and the professionals they encountered throughout their school years. The recollections also carry some implications for the setting that makes a library a pleasant experience for potential users.

Favorable Memories of Libraries

> My memories of my experiences with reading begin at age five with a trip to the public library to get my first library card. I remember having practiced writing my name several times, each time trying to be a little neater than before, so that when the time came for me to sign my library card, they would see this beautiful signature.

> My next remembrance of reading is especially vivid. I recall walking to the public library in my hometown with my "bestest" girl friend. She was much worldlier than I because she already had her very own library card. I remember how big the librarian's desk seemed. I felt very grown up as I gave her my name, address and phone number. I clutched the brown card in my sweaty hand.

> As a small child living in a fairly large community, I loved nothing more than frequent trips to the branch library where I would browse by the hour. The building was a vine-covered, cool, sweet-smelling place and I had a favorite seat in one corner where my girlfriend and I enjoyed many long afternoons. My only problem was selecting only as many books as I could carry home.

The children's department was located in the basement. I remember going to the library with my mother. She would allow me to go downstairs and look at the books while she found her books upstairs. I usually spent my time at a small table that had little chairs around it just my size. Upon this table was a puzzle of the United States. You could fit all the states into a wooden frame correctly by following a picture of the states that always lay beside the puzzle.

As I recall, I received only encouragement for reading. I eagerly awaited the "library day" when we were allowed to select our books for the week. The class would spend half the hour hearing the librarian give short synopses of the new books received and the second half was spent selecting books. As we reached the older grades we were all given the opportunity to work in the library, i.e., stamping books or reshelving them. This, of course, was a new experience and afforded an excellent opportunity to become interested in and acquire knowledge of books and the library.

We moved when I was in fifth grade to a school with a beautiful library. In the summer the library opened on certain days for anybody who wanted to use it. I went regularly, because the school was in walking distance from my house.

We had two old-fashioned bookcases filled with books that comprised the library (rural school). I can remember whizzing through many of them from first grade on. Many were old and probably would be considered poor choices from today's standpoint. As an animal lover I quickly chose and completed the short supply of dog and horse stories. Two which I remember reading were *Silver Chief* and *Justin Morgan Had a Horse* by Marguerite Henry. I rejected most of the so-called classics not because I tried them and disliked them, but because of their torn, tattered condition and dirty yellow pages.

It is in second grade that I recall a specific story, *Goody Two Shoes*. And it was at this time that I got my first library card from the big library downtown. I can still feel the awe at the big room of children's books that were at my disposal — such wealth! And wonder of wonders, I could check out four a week. At first I couldn't decide which four I wanted. It was like being let loose in a candy shop with instructions to help myself to a nickel's worth. I remember one of the four books I chose — *The Life of Christopher Columbus*. I don't remember the other three; no doubt, lighter stuff. Every Saturday, winter and summer, I went to the library as well as using the libraries at school. I continued this through grade school, high school and college.

I have one cherished memory I will always delight in — the day I was allowed a library card, about age twelve. I recall inhaling the smell of the library, glorying in the rows upon rows of books. After I had been granted my card my immediate question was: "How many can I take?"

Books and the public library symbolized freedom for me, because sometimes in the summer my mother would let me take the city bus alone downtown to go to the library.

Shortly after, I was introduced to the best part of school (after learning to read). Tuesday afternoons after school we were allowed to go to the library and browse, dream and wonder. It was fortunate our home was only two blocks from school, for I took as many books as I could carry and could check out . . . . Oddly enough, I didn't confine myself to picture books intended for children my age. I would sit for lengthy periods of time trying to decipher the content of magazines and newspapers.

I'll never forget our library back home. I come from a small farming community and ordinarily such a town doesn't have a very impressive library. However, some wealthy "old timer" saw fit to build an immense grey stone library which occupies nearly a whole block of our small town. It may be that he simply wished to be remembered. Or perhaps he was a lover of knowledge. At any rate his monument has had a profound effect on my life. I used to wander through the rows of book shelves by the hour. It became a ritual with me, like shopping for a new dress. I selected each book very carefully. Looking back, I realize I rarely read more than half of the books I checked out each week. My eyes were bigger than my stomach. Nevertheless, every two weeks, with very good intentions, I'd pick out approximately fifteen books. My choices often amused the librarian. Subject matter ranged from religion to aerodynamics to physics to gardening to philosophy to fiction. Sometimes I'd read only fifty pages from a book; however, amusingly enough, this random reading has been a great help to me as a college student and conversationalist.

In a quiet, nearly closed off section of the R. Public Library and up a short flight of stairs was "my" room. Burgundy velvet curtains, long couches, and leather chairs compelled me to visit the library. The chairs had gold nail heads and I would run my fingers over them as I read. The paneling was dark oak, warm and comfortable with faces in the grain.

The summer my sister was born when I was eleven, I stayed at my aunt's house where there were six cousins and a real treasure house, a Carnegie library. The library was cool and quiet and smelled of books. I read a book a day for six weeks. The infinite variety nearly drove me wild. I wanted to get through all of them. *Girl of the Limberlost* is the one that I remember best from this experience. I finished it while curled up in the bathtub.

In summer time my best friend, J., and I would walk to the library.

The library was far away and by the time we got there we would usually be hot and sweaty. The air conditioning and the books came as great solace. On the way home we would be like the children in the Edward Eager books, as we stopped on church steps under trees to dip into little bits of our books. Then we would usually stop and buy candy and settle in our backyard and read all afternoon.

We moved a lot and the first order of business in each new town was to find the public library and take out a card. Without knowing at that time that I thought so, I can see now that I regarded the library as the one place in every new town where I could find all my old friends: *Little Women, The Little Colonel, The Five Little Peppers* along with that insufferable *Elsie Dinsmore.*

Fifth or sixth grade was a milestone in that each of the five members of my family acquired a book card to the public library in C. Each card allowed the holder to borrow two books per week. I seldom, if ever, got through all ten books, but this was my introduction to the Zane Grey westerns. These were surpassed in my estimation only by his three border stories. I was ecstatic when I found an old bookcase full of Tom Swift books which did not even have to be listed on the cards as part of the two per week quota.

During the summer months the library had a reading program in which I participated. After reading a certain number of books, a summary of which was made for the librarian as each book was returned, the reader was awarded a certificate and a gold star. At the time, I considered my certificate to be a prized possession.

Our public library had a special summer program for a number of years to encourage elementary school children to read. We were given check lists on which to write the names of books we had read. These were then signed by our parents. Prizes were awarded after a certain number of books, usually ten, were read. These prizes became successively more desirable, of course, as the number of books read increased.

It was in the high school library that I began to appreciate the magazine and newspaper. I noticed the differences and variety of this type of media and became a good newspaper and magazine skimmer. I continued reading dog, horse, baseball, adventure and detective stories; however, I used to enjoy walking through the shelves and picking out books that looked good. This is how I found *Cyrano de Bergerac*, which stimulated me to read plays.

At college I worked in the library for part of my tuition. (Up to this time outside reading had been slushy love stories and movie magazines.) There I developed a definite taste for Dickens, Guy de Maupassant, Victor Hugo and again poetry — this time modern collections of little known poets.

I suppose the most memorable experiences of my college career as far as books go have come with the deepening understanding of what they can mean and say to my everyday life. This was somehow symbolized when I acquired a stack permit and wandered behind the guardian desk of the main library for the first time. That was one of the most stirring things I've ever seen. To think that many people have thought they've something significant to say to a world which might or might not listen is somehow awesome to me yet.

Unfavorable Memories of Libraries

In fifth grade I was interested in Greek and Roman mythology, but the school library ran out of books before my curiosity was satisfied. The same thing happened with prehistoric dinosaurs.

At this time the country school closed and I was sent to a parochial school. Each class was allowed to go to the city library once a week. But we could not check out any books without the teacher's approval. This limited us to religious books and simple adventure stories.

Our elementary school library definitely did not deserve its title. We were allowed to check out one book a week, but if everyone did, the room was left bare.

When I went to junior high, I didn't read anything on my own the first year. The library was so much bigger than our grade school library that I was terrified to go in.

My high school library was a closet with old encyclopedias. There was some vague contact with the intimidating public library reference room. To this day I would rather buy a book than go to the library.

Tenth and eleventh grades were spent avoiding the school library. It was dank and sticky — too cluttered for students to move. In 1967 it appeared the same as it had in my aunt's 1920 yearbook.

I scorned the high school library. To begin with, it was located in an abandoned corridor and seemed stocked with romantic novels by the Brontë sisters, who I felt were just not with the events of this modern world.

When I moved from junior high to high school and my library card was transferred to the adult department, I felt pushed up. I wasn't finished there yet and the adult room was ugly and cold.

You could only take out two books at a time so I would sign out two books for me, two books in my mother's name, two in my father's name, two in my grandmother's name thus ending up with eight books.

We moved to Chicago when I was in sixth grade, and I remember my awe and amazement when my father took us downtown to the huge public library. I guess I was so impressed that I would never have even thought of touching one of those books. However, the local library where we lived in the suburbs was smaller and we used to go there regularly on our bicycles.

You entered from either side of the library through big black iron gates and the entry was always dark and damp. There was also a big black bust of a man outside the door and the combination of all these things made the library a scary place. It was spooky going in there.

In those days the children's section of the library was housed in the basement. To reach it one had to descend a steep and poorly lighted stairway and then walk between dark, musty smelling stacks of books. It took courage for a small child to make that trek even when clutching a mother's hand.

At the end of the second grade a frightening thing happened. Our class took a tour through the public library. The most impressive thing about the library was the huge, stuffed bald eagle mounted above the door. It was frightening to look at and seemed so high and unattainable perched over the huge double doors. Inside the smell of books, the sour faced librarian, and the still, quiet atmosphere all seemed as stuffy as the eagle guarding the doorway.

I was never inside a public library until I entered college. I was very frightened to use the library. I was embarrassed to let anyone know I knew so little about a library. However, I soon learned librarians were eager to help and I was amazed at all the things the library had to offer. The main reason I am taking library education as a minor is because I felt a definite lack in my own background of reading. I hope that I can help my students have more memorable and pleasant reading experiences than I had.

Memories of Alternative Libraries

The school library, during the depression days, was one of those "unnecessary" items that school boards felt could be done without. Had it not been for the State Traveling Library and my Dad's trips to Des Moines to transport books to that library in the building across from the state capitol and then back to our school, my reading and that of my schoolmates would have been indeed limited.

I began reading books when our county library sent a collection of books to our sixth grade class. I thought the library was a good excuse for running around the room, so I hung around there regularly. I soon found that some of the books interested me and when I discovered the Hardy Boys mysteries, I was sold.

Later more books became available through a small loan collection from the state library which was kept in the Presbyterian Church where we attended Sunday school.

I went to a country school up to and including the sixth grade. There was a very small library, but I read almost every book available in it. Our teacher always ordered books from the Traveling Library in Des Moines. It was always a big thrill to open the box of books to see what it contained.

From then on the bookmobile, which had a stop about ten blocks from my home, was my access point. Each week I ordered books from my list, they brought them, and I read all the books on ballet, as well as a number of other books which the bookmobile had on its shelves.

Favorable Memories of Librarians

It must have been nearly twenty years since I'd seen that face and when I glanced around I recognized it as surely as if I'd seen it the day before. It was that of the woman who had introduced me to the world of reading. This wonderful lady would sit with me on the cold tile floor of the old library and together we would pull out stacks of books which I could take home and devour.

As I look back there doesn't seem to be any particular plan to my reading which has been extensive. My parents kept a sort of running check on what I read; but now that I think of it, a red-haired librarian by the name of Miss R. probably guided my reading more than anyone. However, she did it so skillfully that I have just now come to realize it. I spent a lot of time in the public library and Miss R. always had a reading suggestion. It sometimes surprised me that the books she suggested were quite good. This is probably how I came to read most of the good books as well as my own selections. I was a prolific reader.

After I had made several trips to the library, Miss B. became aware of the interest in horses that had grown in me and recommended book after book on horses for me to read. I went through all of Walter Farley's books as well as every other book on horses that the library owned.

The librarian had a club in which we, the members, read books and then annotated them and rated them. We did this on 3 x 5 cards which were placed in a file for use by the entire student body.

The person who made me most interested in reading when I was a small child was the town librarian. She must have been very patient with me, for I can remember bothering her very frequently when I was trying to decide which book to take home. I always sought her advice about books, for I knew that she had read every book in the library.

About this time I discovered the public library. Here I spent one to two hours every afternoon. I remember with awe and affection the plump librarian who never shushed, never frowned, who led me constantly to new books. One day she asked me if I knew about gods and goddesses and showed me to the mythology section. I scarcely moved from it for a month.

On the day before registering for high school, my best friends and I returned for a farewell party with the librarian of the children's department. We had been using the adult section for a long time, but now we formally and regretfully closed an era of childhood that had meant much to us through our early life. As we said goodbye, we thumbed through the books that we had read and reread. I lingered especially over the copies of The Little Colonel series, *Anne of Green Gables, The Five Little Peppers* and *Little Women.* What memories those and other books held for me.

Our first trip from camp (army) to town was the occasion for our first trip to the public library. The librarian looked at us in horror, hastily consulted the library board concerning the advisability of checking out books to service personnel, and then became our personal Florence Nightingale.

Unfavorable Memories of Librarians

Our public library failed to lure me down any literary paths. Behind the doors of that formidable building two formidable spinsters guarded the inner sanctum. Nothing more than a hushed footstep ever was heard in that dim hall of horror. Books were kept primly shelved by the spindly spinsters and few had the courage to disturb the neatness, quiet and order that these two not only desired but inflicted.

From the time I learned to read, I read. I can remember having a fight with a librarian over a book about Joan of Arc. She said I was too young, that it was for third graders and I wasn't. I was very stubborn and I read it.

Because of the general dislike for our school librarian, I formed a dislike of the library as well, even though I enjoyed reading. In the fifth grade, I remember that this librarian guided us in a literature unit and she made us read a lot of material written by Kipling, whom to this day I rather dislike.

In sixth grade I was chosen to be a library aid. Out of all the sixth graders there were only three girls chosen so I was really proud. The librarian did her best to make sure that we kept every book on every shelf straight and neat. She stressed this so much that I never once during the entire year checked a book out of that library for myself. I hated to take a book off the shelf, because it messed the shelf up. Consequently, I read very little that year. But I was a good librarian!

The librarian had bad breath and he always tried to interest my friend and me in books that had won Newberry prizes or books of exceptional quality for our age bracket. At the time (grade school) I was more interested in horses, so I generally resisted his efforts. . . . There was one book I took home once to get him off my back. I would still pass up *The Last of the Mohicans* today, because of the extreme pressure I experienced as a youth to read it.

The memory of the librarian at that time is strong. I, of course, had full faith in my ability as a reader. But she continually found it necessary to use her authority and bar me from certain books. This was easily gotten around. I merely asked the older girls to check them out for me. They were actually quite innocent books. I was just supposedly too young.

The library was a project of the women's club and in the particular charge of a Mrs. P., who not only censored the books, but she arbitrarily decided what each patron should be allowed to read. When I tired of the Bobbsey Twins and the Oz books, she was not willing to loan me the more mature books I wanted to try. I got around this by telling her I was getting books for my sister. Since she was nine years older than I, this gave me considerable scope.

Every other Friday our seventh grade teacher would take us to the small, classroom-size school library. Once I heard the librarian scold a boy for talking in the library — that was enough to scare me off from the school library during my two years in junior high school. I browsed about the school library only when I had to write a book report.

The librarian was a sharp tongued ogre whose mere glance threatened my mental health, and being the sensitive, rather insecure child that I was, I found it less traumatic to frequent places other than the library. If a book we wanted to check out didn't suit her fancy, she would read us the riot act with her brows furrowed and her jowls drooping. And consequently, we were actually afraid to try out new types of reading or books we wanted to read because of natural inquisitiveness.

They always wanted to explain the Dewey Decimal system to me rather than let me lay my hands on books. So libraries were a place where books were to be had, but you had better not want them. They made it too difficult for me to want one badly enough. Only mother could get library books without the Dewey Decimal system getting in between.

My problem in adolescent reading was finding something to read. After I had read all the young girl teen stories, I wanted something of the same type on a more adult level. However, I didn't know any titles and didn't know where to go. When I was younger, the children's librarian had been very helpful, but when I graduated to the adult department, the librarians seemed too formidable or else too busy to ask for help.

The summer before I went into high school I remember trying to check out *Hawaii*. I had a big argument with the librarian who said it was too advanced for me. It ended when she called my parents and they said it was O.K.

Located in a new school, the library was a delightful place except for fear of being thrown out. Quite often the oppressive silence was broken by shouts and threats as Mrs. C. marched another offender to the office. One never knew exactly what wrong had been done, so that there seemed some measure of risk involved in asking for a library pass.

The school library was very large and modern, but I never did learn to like it. The stacks of books were arranged in a circular room so that they were all exposed to students studying at the tables in the center of the room. I was no longer able to hide in peace in the rows of books. Two women librarians also created quite a disturbance. They were always yelling at the students to be quiet. The tall thin one was nicknamed "Spoolies," because her hair looked as curly as Shirley Temple's, and the other was called "Fall Turkey," because she certainly wasn't a young chick. After awhile, I just stopped going to the library completely.

Again, I feel that I could have used a little more reading guidance during the junior and senior high school years, because I'm sure I missed some things of which I've no doubt that I was capable. I blame some of this on the high school librarian, who set herself as the absolute arbiter of taste for the young mind. About the most stimulating reading we had on our shelves was Kenneth Roberts, who did light the skies of my sophomore year.

When I was a high school freshman Mrs. W., our librarian, absolutely refused to let me check out *1984*. This spurred me to action. I immediately bought the book and plugged through it just to show her I was old enough to choose my own reading materials.

The high school library had no paperbacks and was run by a woman with a very possessive manner. We were not encouraged to browse through books or to check them out. Also the books, at least as I remember, had no book jackets. Without them they looked old and there was nothing to draw interest to the books.

I was hissed at by the school librarian for asking for a book, *The Hussey*, that was listed as supplementary reading in my history book. It was intimated that I was no better than the title in asking for it.

Reprise

Memories of the thrill of receiving the first public library card are etched into the minds of many of the writers of these autobiographies. Some practiced writing their names in preparation for the big event. A few reported exploring awesome rows of books that they found enchanting. Even in these early years, the writers were frustrated by the limited number of books they were permitted to check out.

For many, early trips to the library are associated with family and friends as companions and sharers of books. Some found special places to read and discovered in the library a sense of security and comfort. We can feel the awe of the one who remembers the burgundy velvet curtains and chairs with gold nail heads. From these early experiences some could even recall special books they discovered: *Little Women,* the Zane Grey westerns, the numerous children's classics. One respondent (and there were dozens of others not included) fondly recalled her pleasure at "story hour" in spite of the floor's hardness, and others related their delight in the prizes given for reading certain numbers of books.

Although just about all of the respondents became regular users of libraries, both school and public, some seem to have done so in spite of a general dislike for the library atmosphere. Some large public libraries were viewed as oppressive, dark, and intimidating. We can picture the black iron gates and the stuffed bald eagle that were perched over huge double doors and that frightened two young children.

Criticism of school libraries centered on their inadequacies. The writers recalled exhausting all too quickly the supply of books on a topic of interest, whether animals or Greek mythology. Some described their school libraries as cluttered and uncomfortable. Others mentioned that the library was in an abandoned hallway or a part of a room used for other activities.

Study participants also complained of the rules for both public and school libraries that demanded absolute silence and that limited the number of books which could be checked out. Others objected to librarians acting as watchdogs over what the young people could or could not read. Remember the youngster who told the person in charge that she was checking out the books for her sister who was nine years older, or the other youngster who had older girlfriends check out books for her? For every obstacle set up by librarians, there is a determined reader who can find ways to get around it. For more than a few, the move from the smaller, cozy children's section to the seemingly impersonal adult one was a difficult adjustment. Even as college students, the respondents found the change from the small, familiar local public library to the large university library to be an intimidating and somewhat threatening experience.

Alternative libraries are given high praise for their part in creating readers. For many readers, church libraries or collections on loan from county or state libraries made books easily accessible. A popular source for books that is mentioned over and over again is the bookmobile. Its usual stop within walking distance of the home is a major attraction; its relatively small size probably makes for a sense of informality and approachability. Users looked forward to browsing through the shelves and requested books that were not on hand to be brought along during the next trip.

Librarians are quite naturally associated with library experiences. For some of our writers, it was a librarian whom they thanked for guidance and for generating enthusiasm over discovering books. Do you recall the librarian in the children's room who sat on the floor and dragged books off the shelves, and then sat with the youngsters and perused them? The successful librarian appears to have a friendly manner, a real knowledge of books, and an understanding of young people's interests. On the other hand, when guidance turns into censorship, however well meaning, the reaction is predictably hostile. At times, this meant discouraging a book choice as inappropriate for the reader's age level or absolutely refusing to allow the person to check out a particular book, seemingly on moral grounds. One can feel the frustration of the reader who was not allowed to progress beyond the Bobbsey Twins and the person intimidated for wanting to check out a book on the supplementary reading list for history.

The image of librarians as rule enforcers is associated with the demand for silence, keeping the books in neat lines on the shelves, and limiting the number of books to be checked out. Occasionally, librarians themselves add to the confusion by talking among themselves and ignoring or, even worse, scolding these patrons. It should be recognized that the libraries of today are seldom operated as they were ten or twenty years ago. And fortunately, for each negative, somewhat stereotypical librarian recalled in the protocols, there were five cheery and knowledgeable ones remembered with gratitude.

11 The Reading of Poetry

Poetry is a form of literature usually cherished by teachers at both the elementary and secondary levels. Yet, in surveys of reading habits and interests, poetry seems of minor importance. Or is it?

Surprisingly, in wallets and handbags across America, there are often ragged copies of a verse or two, cut from a newspaper or magazine. Sometimes a poem may appear in the "Dear ____" columns of daily newspapers which reflect a common emotion or experience. Most ceremonial occasions include the reading or writing of a poem or two. For birthdays and gift days, a not inconsiderable number of people pen a verse or send a card imprinted with a poem in order to express their sentiment. Perhaps this type of writing is not really poetry, at least not the kind that teachers discuss and dissect in the classroom; but the instinct for sentiment in rhythmic language is recognized as important by most people.

It is noteworthy that poetry was mentioned more often in the protocols from the 1960s than in those from the 1970s. In the 1980s, still fewer respondents recorded the reading of poems as a part of their experience with literature. Perhaps it was sheer accident that no one thought to mention poetry, or perhaps the lack of mention indicates a real decline in the reading of it. But whether the reading of poetry is on the rise or the decline, what the respondents experienced while reading poetry as they grew up has interesting implications about the present-day status of poetry in our culture.

Early Years

When I was quite small my mother read to me a great deal. She read poems to me and I give her credit to this day for the fact that I always liked poetry even though my contemporaries were dead set against it.

My father loved poetry and he tried to instill this in me at an early age. He began reading simple poems to me before I started school and gradually worked up to more complicated ones. He never required that I memorize these poems, but somehow this

121

seemed to come naturally. I enjoyed these sessions very much. We would talk over the poems we read and Daddy always wanted to know how a certain poem made me feel or why I liked it.

Speaking of my dad, I think he was the biggest influence in my attitude toward poetry. He could recite great quantities of it from memory, and I decided I would match him in quantity. I memorized much of the poetry we studied in high school, much to the amazement of my teachers. Longfellow, Lowell, Dickinson, and Robert Frost were my first favorites, and I can still recite much of what I learned then, the rest coming back with a brief review.

One of the first books that I owned was a small volume of poetry which was given to me by my grandmother. I read and reread this little book and still love the poems that it contained.

I still go back to a poetry collection called *Through Many Colored Glasses*. Inside are poems such as "The Animal Fair," "Stars" and Blake's mysterious, "The Tiger." All were complete with fine illustrations.

Elementary and Junior High School

We used to dramatize poems on our own too (although this was before high school) without any teacher help. "Horatius at the Bridge" was one of our favorites. "Evangeline" and "The Highway Man" were others I remember memorizing long passages from and acting them out on our way home from school or at home itself.

Poems were "learned-by-heart." "The Inchcape Rock," "Which Shall It Be," "The Village Blacksmith" and numerous others became a part of our memory store. A last line from the last page of an early reader: "Great oaks from little acorns grow," so impressed me that the accompanying picture is still vivid in my memory.

I liked reading poetry and committing it to memory. Before I finished the 8th grade, I had committed to memory the *One Hundred and One Best Poems*. This was not in connection with any school work.

Although I always enjoyed a good story, the pull of the didactic poem was ever present. When a cousin came and brought *Gone With the Wind*, I read that book and other Civil War stories. But reading, studying and memorizing poetry were always more pleasant for me than reading the stories. An adult friend gave me *A Book of Living Poems*, and I learned Miriam Teicher's "Awareness," the opening verses of Wordsworth's "Intimations of Immortality," and the closing lines of Tennyson's "Ulysses." These morally instructive poems were useful for YWCA and Sunday school programs.

From the first time in grade school that I had to stand before the class and recite "Oh, Captain, My Captain" I formed a dislike for poetry.

I was quite a chatterbox and in the fourth grade every time I was caught talking out of turn, I was required to memorize and recite poetry. To this day I hate "Barbara Frietchie."

In junior high English I had to memorize "Snow Bound." We spent almost a full nine weeks listening to each other recite what we'd memorized. Poetry immediately became the ugliest thing that I could ever imagine. It took a modern poetry course in college to change my mind.

In eighth grade we studied Sandburg. The entire class snickered through "Chicago" which enraged the teacher so much that we were forced to memorize and recite it out loud. I found this extremely distasteful. In fact, I have never gotten over my dislike of Sandburg.

In the 7th or 8th grade we had to memorize a poem. I learned "Charge of the Light Brigade" and to this day I can still recite most of it. By the time half the class had recited "I remember, I remember" everyone else remembered it too.

It was about this time that poetry began to appeal to me. Our family library contained a suede leather bound book of Longfellow's poems. The cover was simply delightful to the touch and contrary to the old adage, I did judge the book by the cover.

High School

I do recall a fondness for poetry about this time. At summer camp we had poetry study and I fell in love with the very lovely and beautiful woman who taught it. I am thankful that at this impressionable age that I was introduced to the wonderful field of poetry and that my fondness for it never dwindled but increases as time goes on.

My love of poetry started in my junior year of high school when I fell under the influence of the English teacher mentioned earlier in this paper. Poetry had not been my favorite material since my junior hi days when our class sat for hours reading "Snow Bound" and "Evangeline," and "Courtship of Miles Standish." To this day I dislike these poems.

During my sophomore year in high school I acquired a sudden interest in poetry. This was due to my brother's having "made the headlines" in a small newspaper of a small Nebraska college town where he was a student. My brother had written several short poems and it was then and there that a "youthful poet" had been discovered. This aroused me. I read and memorized a great deal of poetry during my high school years. Favorite poets were Longfellow, Bryant, Kipling, Byron and Whitman. (Kipling's "If" gripped me so much that I wrote Kipling endeavoring to get his autograph.) I was pleased to receive his autograph together with the words, "Greetings to the Young American." Regretfully I say that I have misplaced it.

Most of my real enjoyment in poetry and literature developed from declamatory and interpretive reading. I truly enjoy reading a poem aloud and I believe most poetry should be read aloud to fully appreciate it.

That same year (high school junior) a creative writing course aroused my interest in poetry. The individual who instilled a love of poetry in me was the junior English teacher. She concentrated on poetry and loved it so much (soundly, not gushily) that this appreciation communicated itself to us. We read *The Iliad, The Odyssey, Enoch Arden, The Rime of the Ancient Mariner.* She tried to make us philosophize about life in our discussions of poetry. I can clearly visualize her face as she led us in our interpretation of Elizabeth Barrett Browning's poem, "How Do I Love Thee?" We sat there and giggled — yet we knew she was happily married. In spite of our embarrassment, I feel that many of her students took away much thought for future consideration. Several classmates and I prided ourselves in being able to spout poetry on occasion. And more than one recess period was devoted to a guessing game of "What Poem is This?"

A lawyer friend of the family often read to me the poems of Longfellow and Riley, so that I cannot remember a time when I didn't like poetry. As a senior in high school I was sent to interview the poet named Lew Sarett and to report his program. My interest in poetry soared again. I sought out volumes of lyrics, especially those of Sara Teasdale. At least I avoided the clutches of Edgar Guest.

An even more meaningful experience in twelfth grade, however, was my first real feeling for poetry. This came through an assignment where Mrs. G. had me read Milton's *Paradise Lost* in its entirety. I became very interested in Milton, even memorizing his sonnet "On His Blindness." Shelley and Keats, Byron, Browning and Shakespeare became more than names to be memorized.

The third (memorable experience with books) was *The Winged Horse* read at the onset of my second semester as a senior. I was preparing for scholarship examinations and I think some teacher recommended it. I read almost all the night. Chaucer, Milton,

Shelley, Byron, Keats, above all Keats. I discovered them as people, in any case, if not as poets, quite by myself in this wonderful book, in a happy-making brush with literature that never has had a parallel, for all I have read since.

But in my last two years of high school, I was exposed to great American and British poets in a different way. We read them just as we had read these other poems in Junior high, but there was something added that had been missing for the earlier poems, and I believe it was the teacher. Somehow he was able to make these poems more than specific patterns of words which rhymed abab. When he read them, they came alive — they were life. They opened up the secrets of life only to enclose them in darker secrets, but this did not discourage our interest in them. I believe my ambition to become an English teacher was born at this time, although I did not realize it then.

Poetry in great amounts entered my world once again (highschool). At first willingly, but as time passed, it became the mill stone about my neck. Memorization had taken over in poetry and "compelled" memorization without regard to oral interpretation seemed most unpalatable to me at this time. Where once "Daf-fodils" had been read beneath the covers with the aid of a flashlight, now I felt only disgust and dislike of poetry.

But when it became necessary to interpret the meaning of each line of a poem and decide how the author felt when writing it and why he expressed himself as he did — I rebelled! I love poetry for its meaning (in its entirety), its rhythm and its sheer beauty, but I do not believe it should be torn asunder.

One of my high school teachers always stressed meter in poetry. Now I have to concentrate to read poetry for meaning. I get involved with beat and lose the message.

Poetry never appealed to me. I lost all enjoyment as a result of a detailed analysis of each poem. The meaning of the whole seemed to be lost to the study of minute parts. I remember winding up with a series of unrelated symbols and being unable to see the relationships between them.

In this literature course, we studied poetry also. I left the works of the Romantic poets such as Wordsworth, Keats, Coleridge, and Lord Byron with the feeling that there was no poetry or prose ever written which could match theirs for beauty, style or thought-provoking theme. This course has been invaluable to my subsequent college work.

In my senior year of high school and on into college, the "music" of the English poets all the way from Chaucer to the American Robert Frost enchanted me. The turn of a phrase, the imagery, and the "puzzle" in a poem were a challenge and something quite marvelous.

In the realm of poetry Poe and Longfellow, my junior hi favorites, were considered "out." Eliot was "in." e.e. cummings was "in." Dylan Thomas was "in." Although I read and enjoyed to a degree these three poets, I thought that none surpassed Stephen Crane.

College and Adult

My real enjoyment of poetry began in these years when I had a literature teacher who read poems beautifully. When I learned to analyze poetry, I began to understand and enjoy it. . . . During my college years I particularly liked English poets, especially the modern poets. I became a loyal reader of T. S. Eliot and I enjoyed Wilde, Wordsworth and even Chaucer. . . . When I began to write poetry, I seemed to imitate the styles of Whitman and Eliot. I liked writing highly descriptive poems with understated messages. (I won 4th place in an International Poetry Contest in 1959 with a poem of this type.) College awakened in me an interest in modern poetry, a real understanding of Shakespeare and interest in reading plays and seeing them performed.

My college literature courses were instrumental in leading me into an entirely different avenue of reading interest. For the first time in my life it occurred to me that poetry had just as much to offer as novels and short stories. Robinson Jeffers, whose pen could turn words and phrases into nature scenes that were poetically capable of placing one in the midst of a perfectly painted mountain range, was a poet that I developed a strong attachment for. From Robinson Jeffers' poetry, I turned to poets such as Edna St. Vincent Millay and D. H. Lawrence. Both of these poets, who represented the finest in the school of "imagery," were my favorites. T. S. Eliot's profound, but cynical works gained my attention in college also. Eliot's technical excellence and his belief that the emotion of art was impersonal, probably discouraged many from reading him. I found that while Eliot wasn't particularly concerned about the kind of reader who might only appreciate an Edgar A. Guest, he gave me many occasions to ponder over his impregnated thoughts . . . buried so deep in his poetry that it took a fine tooth "mental comb" to extract them.

About the time of high school graduation and the first year of college, like the other girls, I became very enamored of *The Prophet*, Kahlil Gibran, and the *Rubaiyat of Omar Khayyam.* The somewhat dreamy philosophy appealed to us as being sophisticated and we pondered the beauty of the well-turned phrases. To this day these books attract me and I like to pick up one or the other and read a paragraph. Poetry also came to be more attractive in a hit and miss sort of way.

I have always loved poetry though my favorites are probably not considered in fashionable good taste. Oh, I like T. S. Eliot and Dylan Thomas, but I'm also very fond of some of Rupert Brooke's poetry as well as Edna St. Vincent Millay's and Sara Teasdale's, simply because their poetry sounds so pretty and isn't afraid to carry a simple message. And I cherish my *Collected Poems of Carl Sandburg* which my cherubs gave me for a Christmas present.

Pilot days overseas allowed free time; and some of this time was devoted to the books, frequently sex-slanted paperbacks, that circulated around the squadron. Curiously enough, there were some good poetry anthologies in the outfit which seemed to offer a nice change of pace. Some poetry seemed to hold attraction for all.

Reprise

Young people are influenced early on to read poetry after hearing a favorite adult read verse aloud — much in the same way they are influenced to read fiction after hearing it read aloud. To be sure, the oral reading of poetry is reported less frequently in the protocols than is the oral reading of prose. Parents, grandmothers, and an occasional family friend are mentioned as reading poetry aloud. These persons seemed to be people who, themselves, liked poetry and who had memorized a great number of poems and could recite them. Often, the poetry was an eclectic hodgepodge far beyond the scope of the youngster to whom it was read. Instances are cited where it became a kind of challenge to the young reader to match the mentor's knowledge of poetry. The writers mention that, later in their lives, camp counselors and also English teachers seemed to exert considerable influence in building their appreciation of poetry.

Sometimes a respondent's appreciation of poetry came about as a result of a "backdoor" approach: poetry was a necessary vehicle for speech or elocution lessons or as material for dramatic presentations. One person mentioned a creative writing class as opening the door to an appreciation of poetry. Through attempting to write, the respondents came to an understanding of what others did so superbly.

A few individuals mentioned a favorite book of poetry that had been given to them as their very own. Often, these volumes remained with them into adult life and are still turned to as one turns to an old friend. In some cases, poems were read so often that they were finally memorized. In one case, an individual could still remember the illustration for a particular poem because the poem had made such an impact that the picture became memorable as well. Another writer remembered the feel of the binding of a well-loved book of poetry. The love of poetry, therefore, focuses upon not only individual poems, but also on aesthetic experience involving the visual and kinesthetic sense of the reader.

The old, standard poems seem to be more memorable than the contemporary ones. The writers speak of memorizing and loving Poe, Longfellow, Whittier, and Frost. Some even mention the fascination that patriotic and didactic poems held for them. Although these students came across people like Eliot, Thomas, and Yeats later in life, they admit to a preference for the earlier writers: Longfellow, Whittier, and Keats. This would seem to indicate that the poetry to which they were exposed in their early years actually formed their tastes.

The memorization of poetry is frequently mentioned, sometimes favorably, other times unfavorably. It was a joy to those who seemed to do it unconsciously and to those who saw it as a challenge. But memorization was anathema to the majority when it was a forced assignment. However, one senses, in some autobiographies, a grudging admiration for those individuals who acquired a storehouse of memorized poetry. People seem to admire the "poetry-stocked" mind just as they admire the multilingual mind.

Surprisingly, there are few comments about what poetry does to or for the reader. One person recognized the subtle pleasure that comes from images wrapped in rhythmic language. Another mentioned how poetry unlocks a body of ideas and feelings. Yet, from all these samples, one gathers that poetry provides only a momentary sensation. It is most like an incantation rather than an epiphany that influences one's thoughts or actions. It might be compared to a delicate crystal ball that mesmerizes us momentarily with its brilliant flashes of light, triggering an emotional or mental response. But then, it is quickly forgotten, to be remembered only when similar lights flash again across one's mind.

12 The Classics

The protocols are filled with references to that standard reservoir of literature, "the classics." In this group are those books usually written before, or at least early in, the twentieth century which are considered the backbone of a literary education. Some titles, such as *Hans Brinker, Alice in Wonderland,* and *Little Women,* are thought of as "children's classics." These appear in the overview of elementary reading and in the chapter on oral reading. Almost without exception, these books provide rich, enjoyable reading experiences for the young.

Literary education in the secondary schools has been built largely on the presentation of the classics. Back in the 1890s, the Committee on Uniform College Entrance Requirements picked a limited number of books over which high school students were to be examined for college entrance. These became the dominant body of material in the literary curriculum and, to this day, are still thought to be fundamental to *basic* education.

Most suggestions for improving education usually call for a reinstatement of many of these titles and certainly endorse the philosophic stance behind their selection. The proponents of this curriculum believe that the struggle with these titles will ultimately produce some real educational benefits for the teenager. Hence, it is interesting to ferret out the reaction to the classics by this group of people — people who ultimately became sufficiently interested in reading to make its promotion a part of their vocational endeavor. And remember that the writers of the autobiographies are predominantly English teachers or librarians.

The first and most important volumes in the classics are the works of Shakespeare. Almost everyone had had some exposure to his plays. So let us start with those and see the respondents' varied reactions to their reading of the plays as high school and college students, and then move on to both positive and negative statements about some of the other classics.

Shakespeare

A favorite aunt introduced me to Charles and Mary Lamb's *Tales from Shakespeare.* This led me to an early concept of classical literature. Shakespeare remains today as my favorite.

In the eighth grade, I and my classmates received a dose of Shakespeare which seemed a bit much at the time. We each had to make Shakespeare notebooks (a semester long project) and the competition to produce the handsomest cover was terrific. In retrospect, it seems we were more concerned with the covers than the contents. One thing about all this was that it was in contrast to my passion for reading about the talented Tom Swift.

I began to like Shakespeare only after the movie, *Julius Caesar,* with James Mason and Marlon Brando came out, and I concluded plays were better seen then read.

I was never really involved with Shakespeare. We read all of the usual plays, but the analysis killed it for me. *Romeo and Juliet* became interesting only after I saw the movie.

My first introduction to Shakespeare was *Romeo and Juliet* in ninth grade and there started a love affair with Shakespeare's plays. I loved to listen to our teacher read it aloud. The lines with the strange combination of words were beautiful. And if you were sharp and listened well, you could pick up things that were downright funny.

A second teacher, early in high school, introduced me to the reading of Shakespeare plays with the reading and dramatization of *Julius Caesar.* This led to a devouring of anything Shakespearean for several years.

A class in English literature during my senior year of high school broadened my interests considerably. For me, the most exciting reading occurred during our study of Shakespeare. I had read *Othello* and *Hamlet* when I was about thirteen, but they meant almost nothing in comparison to the understanding I gained during that second encounter.

I was greatly impressed with *Macbeth*. In this work came my most exciting discoveries. I can even remember how the classroom looked when I discovered how Birnham woods did come and why Macduff was not of woman born. I was so impressed that I decided that day to become an English teacher.

I recall studying *Julius Caesar, Macbeth,* and *As You Like It.* Most high school students at the time had an intense dislike for Shakespeare. However, I enjoyed the plays. The particular English teacher I had at the time also was the drama coach, and although I hated school plays and still do, she did a magnificent job with Shakespeare's characters.

We were very fortunate during our high school days to have an English teacher come to our small school who loved the works of Shakespeare and other great masters. Under her expert guidance, the characters came to life for us. However, when I attempted to read them without her supervision and interpretation, the great works had little meaning for me.

I hated almost all the books we studied in English classes. After having spent nine weeks reading *Macbeth* aloud in twelfth grade English, I'm still not fond of Shakespeare. We read a lot of Dickens in high school and I never liked him either. I hated Charlotte Brontë the most. I was to read *Jane Eyre* for a seventh grade book report, but I couldn't finish it and have never been able to force myself to try it again.

In high school I frankly hated Shakespeare. I skimmed through the assignments but certainly did not enjoy them. It wasn't until I took an excellent Shakespeare course in college that I really learned to appreciate his works and enjoy reading them.

My faculty adviser was head of the English Department (College). Since he planned to retire at the end of my sophomore year, he was determined to have me in his two Shakespeare courses, even though they were limited to seniors. The Shakespeare courses were the most interesting of my college years. I could hardly wait for class time.

Shakespeare in high school bored me, but when Father K. taught it at Ambrose College, it was dynamite. *Hamlet* was my favorite play. I came to understand the makings of a tragic hero.

Other Classics

In about sixth grade, I had a teacher who on every Friday would read to us from Dickens or Kipling. In this manner I was introduced to *Nicholas Nickleby, A Christmas Carol, Great Expectations, The Jungle Book* and *Kim.* Of course, these tastes simply whetted my appetite to dine more deeply in these two authors.

I well remember despising "The Legend of Sleepy Hollow" as we paraphrased and outlined our way through every chapter.

High school literature classes were disappointing at first. Does anyone really enjoy reading *Silas Marner?* I can remember only one thing from reading that novel — I distinctly remember wishing George Eliot had never been born. I had a similar distaste for *The Odyssey.*

It was during the high school years that I became somewhat aware of author prestige. A book I wished to read was not on the reading list, but when I asked the teacher if it would be acceptable, her answer was, "Yes, any book by John Galsworthy is acceptable." Strange, now I can't remember which book it was.

I think the most non-pleasurable reading I had was Dickens' *A*

Christmas Carol. (This is correct only if you exclude *Lord Jim* which I read as a freshman in college.) The reason I acquired an antipathy toward this charming tale is due to the fact that we studied the story, acted the play, heard the record, and saw the movie. After this intensive study I felt as if I had eaten the entire goose purchased by Scrooge. Somehow after "God bless us everyone" in all mediums I was no longer a Tiny Tim fan.

During my high school days, I read most of the classroom assignments, but was bored by the masterpieces, or perhaps I failed to understand them. They seemed to be written in another language and seemed not to entertain, but confuse.

The Count of Monte Cristo represents a milestone in my life for I learned, suddenly it seemed, that I was reading rather difficult things and was not bored with them.

As I grew older, I reveled in such books as *Little Women, The Five Little Peppers,* Campfire Girl stories . . . any book with a good down-to-earth story. I truly could have improved Longfellow's ending and have Evangeline find her lover before he is dying. I even read *The Odyssey, The Merchant of Venice* and *The Great Stone Face* with enjoyment. I tried to read *David Copperfield* and *A Tale of Two Cities* as an adolescent, but they were too cumbersome.

Somehow I seem to recall that most of my literature classes were spent rehashing the same material for days, while I wanted to go on to the next story.

One interesting development during this time was that I went back to some of the classics from the book club and read again those I'd given up in my junior high days. One of these was *Wuthering Heights* and it became a favorite. On the other hand, when I finally made it through *The Scarlet Letter,* I decided I was smarter in the first place to have quit after the first few pages.

In the ninth grade I was exposed to the classics by my English teacher. I read *Jane Eyre* and became so involved in it that several mornings I read until four a.m. It was so cold in my room that winter that I used to read with wool mittens on. After writing detailed book reports we were supposed to read the novel again to see what we learned the second time. . . . I didn't.

When I was a junior I read *War and Peace.* Because it is a very long book, written to be read at leisure, I decided to completely take my time when I read it. It took almost a month to finish it, reading two or three other much shorter books for book reports at the same time. I read *War and Peace* only when I had time to sit down and enjoy it fully. In this way I formed a curious attachment to that book which still exists. I got to know it, we spent a lot of time together, and somehow this book and I became "friends." I think that our friendship is unique — a product of the books content and of the manner in which I read it — and I think that we will remain friends through many more readings.

Generally speaking, English teachers who insisted on the memorization of parts of *The Rime of the Ancient Mariner* or who were concerned that I "get" the meaning of Shakespeare and Addison began to bore and irritate me to the point that I almost came to believe that the great works of literature were creations devised by authors for the sole purpose of torturing young students. Most of the fun and sense of wonder from reading had deserted me and consequently, the scope and the depth of what reading I did independently was not appreciably expanded.

In eleventh grade I was exposed to Emerson and Thoreau, but I didn't understand them until I read them in college.

I date my introduction to literature as a really satisfying intellectual challenge in addition to its entertainment value to an elective English course in my high school in which we studied *Heart of Darkness* and several other mind probing works. I remember being astounded that there was so much significance beneath the literal quality of Conrad's story.

Books required by my high school English course really turned me off. *Huckleberry Finn*, *The Scarlet Letter* and books by Hemingway, Faulkner and Camus were picked apart week after week. The symbolism in the books I really liked if I noticed it myself, but the constant "see this" and "see that" ruined many good books for me. Such books as *The Pearl* and *Siddhartha* were books I liked at that age merely because I saw the symbolism MYSELF.

A third memory from my high school years was my introduction to Ancient Greek literature and Shakespeare. Although I can recall spending a great deal of time on the former, I had great difficulty in reading it and therefore disliked it immensely. This dislike lasted into college when I was assigned *The Odyssey* and *The Iliad* for a second time. Although I arrived at a better understanding this second time, I could not rid myself of my basic dislike for it.

Another memory I have from my high school years was my introduction and subsequent dislike of Russian literature. I was assigned, over a course of time, *Crime and Punishment* and *The Brothers Karamazov*. I can recall having to make a list, usually very long, of characters, which were always very long and quite unpronounceable, to keep by my side as I read.

Another teacher undid as much or more than the one who aroused my interest. He forced certain classics upon us such as Dickens and slowed my wanting to read on my own and made me want to read lazy type books, ones that didn't take much effort.

One thing I never did understand even though I read it and wrote a paper on it was a novel by Thomas Wolfe: *Of Time and the River.* It seemed that my English teachers weren't too concerned about what I got out of my readings, just that I did them.

I have never regretted reading a book, for I find each a new experience whether it becomes a favorite or not. If I can't get into a book on the first few tries, I give up and wait for a couple of years to pass. I remember especially doing this with two books, *Anna Karenina* and *Jean Christophe* . . . . So far I still haven't had the courage to pick them up.

I enjoyed reading about the seventeenth century lyrics because I think it was during that course that the realization came to me that literature is a reflection of the life of the times — that it is complementary to history.

I read all the classics forced upon us in English classes. I hated every one when I began it, but loved each one by the end.

In college I learned to analyze everything I read. When reading supposedly for pleasure, I still find myself looking at plot structure, details and character types. However, I am regaining, I think, the love of reading I had when I was very young.

Independent reading in the college English class was supervised by the teacher. I recall my indignation when told I wasn't ready for *Anna Karenina* and assigned *The Forsythe Saga.*

I spent entirely too much time reading the complete works of Shakespeare and Tolstoy. I became a reading snob and lost all desire to read in high school. Only one teacher presented reading to me in a class where I was really ready (11th grade), *A Tale of Two Cities.*

In high school for the most part I read literature of which I had heard and knew to be adult. Many times I had to give up the battle of wading through books I was too immature to really appreciate. I really surprised myself by actually enjoying *War and Peace* in the eleventh grade. The reading of this book was my major accomplishment of the year.

Much of the pushing I did to read advanced literature was due to my older sister and an older friend who both read avidly. I tried to gear my reading tastes to theirs, but finally began developing my own. Another reason for reading on a high level is, of course, a striving for peer status.

I have definite blocks in connection with literature which I know to be *good literature* and which I therefore do not want to read. If I know that a book is a classic, I find many reasons for not reading it until I have to. I then read it, and once I have overcome the hazard of knowing I HAVE to, I often enjoy it. What I do not

know is why I have to force myself to read classics. Something
rises up and stands between me and such a book and says; "You
SHOULD read this, but let's not."

Reprise

The salient impression about reading of the classics in these protocols
is that "one person's meat is another person's poison." Some loved
Romeo and Juliet while others could not abide it. Some enjoyed *Silas
Marner* while others detested it. Generally the responses were favorable
to romances such as *Jane Eyre* or *Pride and Prejudice* and to adventure
stories such as *The Count of Monte Cristo*. As teenagers, the respondents
seemed to enjoy those classic works with content that corresponds to
adolescent reading interests.

Some of the readers who enjoyed the classics often mentioned that
their interest in them stemmed from a retelling of the tale. One points
out that reading Lamb's *Tales from Shakespeare* led to a lifelong interest
in Shakespeare's works. Several mention that motion picture produc-
tions, filmstrips, and dramatizations inspired them to read the actual
book. A teacher's real enthusiasm for a work may be transmitted to
some of the students; this is the emotive school of criticism and of
literary pedagogy. Perhaps the students react more to the teacher than
to the work itself.

It seems fairly clear that most of these people's taste had to reach
a certain level of maturity before the classics were appreciated. Some
mention their senior high school English classes as being responsible
for their interest in the classics, but more often, it was not until their
college English courses that they began to understand the reasons for
labeling a literary work as "classic." Even then, some respondents had
been so traumatized by their earlier exposure to a particular title that
they could never overcome their distaste for it.

What, then, were the teaching techniques that instilled in students
a long-lasting dislike for a classic? Dissecting the work paragraph by
paragraph is one of the approaches that is commonly mentioned. This
is implied throughout the bulk of the autobiographies by recurring
expressions such as: "tearing the work apart," "symbol hunting,"
"getting the meaning," and "reading line by line slowly." A number
of the writers complained about spending much too much time on a
single work, on memorization, and on having to outline the work or
make vocabulary lists. Students responded more favorably when they
were permitted to read at their own pace, simply enjoying a book and
figuring out meanings or discovering symbols for themselves. Ob-

viously, this implies an inductive method of teaching beyond the practice of today's teachers.

There are hints that many of those who liked the classics did so for approval; there seemed to be a certain "snob appeal" in being able to report that they had read this type of book. Others felt that reading the classics made them appear more mature than their peers. Sometimes, those readers who did not like the classics evidenced a certain guilt because of their dislike, a guilt and rejection that they carried with them into adult life.

Most of the protocols indicate a feeling that the classics were thrust at the writers willy-nilly in the public schools, without consideration of the students' age or interests. On the other hand, most of the respondents might never have known this body of literature without the school program, for only rarely did a parent or a friend influence these young people to read the classics. Additionally, literary societies like those rampant in Victorian times, such as the Tennyson or Browning or Shakespeare clubs, which stimulated interest in particular writers, virtually do not exist today. Only the "great book" courses still continue to survive in some colleges and local recreational classes.

The protocols seem to imply that American literary programs in the secondary schools are still built from the reservoir of adult classics set up in the nineteenth century. Often, these programs are presented as early as junior high school. Senior year programs in high school are almost exclusively built on this body of literature. The major objective of secondary programs becomes clear: to see that young people have read certain selections before they graduate. Evidently, knowing a few of Shakespeare's plays is considered as fundamental to one's education as knowing the multiplication tables. At the same time, teachers profess that, by presenting the classics, they are really increasing reading enthusiasm for and an appreciation of the great works of literature. It is quite disturbing to find that the protocols indicate exactly the opposite situation for many of the young.

13 Barriers: Why People Don't Read

Even among this select group of people, whose choice of profession would indicate an interest in reading, there were some who admitted, frankly, that they could not be called "readers." Some of the writers reported that they were never hooked on reading, and others said that they became unenthusiastic readers at a certain period in their youth. Several did not discover reading until college or adult life. Most indicated a kind of shame as they confessed their lack of enthusiasm, which was created, perhaps, by the fact that they were in a profession that promoted reading. These individuals found it almost mandatory to seek reasons for their lack of an affinity for reading. With all this in mind, it seems important to examine what brought about their aversion to reading: was it something within themselves or was it due to a series of happenings along the way?

The protocols that follow are presented in a rough chronological pattern beginning with the elementary school period and moving on to the college period. Here, in their own words, are the explanations of what prevented these people from becoming readers.

Elementary Years

After I began grade school my interest in reading and books decreased as my other interests broadened. At this time the emphasis on reading at home decreased also and before I realized it, television had completely taken the place of books. I can remember reading circles in grade school with each taking his turn, but after school was over I had so many other things I wanted to do.

I also remember my parents constantly "telling" me I was a poor reader and would never do well. Being told this, I believed it and never bothered to do much "outside reading." (comics etc.) I do remember reading a hard-bound copy of *Donald Duck* in which I received much pleasure because it was a real "hard-bound" grown-up looking book to me. From the sixth grade on not much was said about my reading — by that time we all avoided the distasteful subject.

Periodic, terrific headaches entered the picture even though I began wearing glasses at the age of seven. Consequently, I avoided anything but definitely assigned public school and Sunday school assignments. This situation continued through high school when I was hospitalized for several months. Following a period of convalescence, I entered almost a different world, one of reading for pleasure as well as for curiosity.

I continued this avid interest in reading until I was in fifth grade. Then the one-eyed monster, commonly known as television, entered the realms of our living room. My reading life conformed to watching cartoon shows and horror movies that gave me nightmares. To say the least, the television set replaced any book. I hated to admit it, but this involvement with the one-eyed monster continued until I entered high school.

Until then, I read only what was required and often neglected to do that.

As soon as I was progressing through the primary grades I remember a distinct lack of enthusiasm for reading because my mother tried to force books on me which I disliked, either because they were too difficult or they were about subject matter in which I had no interest. My older sister had been extremely fond of horse stories and I could not tolerate them.

In junior high my parents were continually pushing my reading, but made no concrete suggestions — consequently, I did not read . . . out of spite.

Something happened in fourth grade. I lost interest in books. My teacher was impatient and embarrassed me before the class for reading too slowly and not being able to retell the contents of the material. How could I? All my attention was on her and what she might say in way of comment. I became frustrated, lost all desire for reading at home or library, I was worried about promotion. I "dragged" through the term and cried for relief.

After I had become acquainted with reading in the elementary schools, I lost interest in books. Our reading assignments were by one page at a time no matter how long the story. In the third grade we spent 25 days, counting repeats, on *The Nuremberg Stove* and to this day I couldn't tell you what it was about. If you stuttered on one word, you had to read the page over. Under fear and tension, we attempted to read.

In my grade school days, I was never stimulated to read as the book supply was terrible. I went to a country school in which books never changed. New books were just unheard of. By the time I was in the sixth or seventh grade, I had read every book in the bookcase.

As a child I don't remember ever being motivated to read. My grades, both in elementary and secondary in reading were always above average, but I never picked up a book on my own and just read for pleasure or information.

I do know that in my first four years of elementary school my parents moved seven times. Thus, I went to seven different schools in Colorado in grades one through four. The only area that was damaged by these seven changes was that of *reading*. In one school I would be taught to sight read and four months later move to another school where I would be told to sound out the word. Also each school would be at a different level of reading material. Thus, on occasion, I would be placed in an advanced reading class when I actually had limited ability. Finally in the fifth grade I was placed in a remedial reading class and almost started all over again in learning to read. The process I was then taught was sight reading.

My father has always read quite a bit, but my mother doesn't. She is very social and talkative — so I found that I enjoyed talking with her more than reading. This was nurtured when I was young and has carried over.

I did not read for pleasure when I was a youngster. I read well in school, and looked the part of a bookworm — thick glasses, prim braids, braces — but libraries did not interest me as did dolls, kick-the-can and draw-a-round circle.

There were always inducements offered to make a child read. There were summer reading clubs with prizes for the highest quantity of books read and later, certificates and gold seals in upper elementary school for reading and reporting on ten books a year. I always enrolled, because it was the socially accepted thing to do. I never finished because books were for school, and running, jumping and playing was for fun.

When I was a child I was too busy to read. I could not sit long enough to get interested in a book. My mother tried to encourage me to read. She even took me to the neighborhood public library three times a week for an hour or so. I only looked at pictures and easier books while there.

Along about this time also, my left eye was operated on so all the more I read less and less.

Junior High School Years

During the summers I worked in the school office and helped unpack and consequently read some of the new books. This should have stimulated me a great deal. It did during the summer, but with the onset of school in the fall, the interest became inactive. I think that unconsciously I came to believe myself a rather slow reader and decided that since it took so long to finish a book and since I had so many other things to do, I didn't have time to read. Entering here also is the fact that there was little required reading for me in the classroom during these years. What reading I did was completely on my own motivation.

Seventh grade remains as a low-tide mark in my early reading experiences, since at that time I was deprived of the privilege of using the classroom library as a punishment for reading books during class instruction. Concomitant with this, our family had increased in size and together with the rebuff I had received in seventh grade and the additional domestic responsibilities which devolved on me while at home, I gradually decreased my reading and this reached its nadir in my secondary educational years at which time I did absolutely no outside reading in school or at home.

My interest, even during my grammar and high school days, in reading was very limited. In our household, work was first and books were secondary. The only book my parents read was the Bible. They did not subscribe to any of the popular periodicals nor did they visit the public library. The few books in our home consisted of school textbooks and a few books concerning religion.

While I was in grammar school and high school I never had a reading interest. I cannot remember any of my teachers trying to influence me to read, nor can I remember my parents trying to influence me. My parents kept one book at all times in their house and that was the Bible. We did have a few Bible storybooks, but somehow I was not interested in reading them, because I had been told the stories in church.

When I reached junior high age, my outside reading began to decline and my social life took a turn for the better. I still enjoyed reading, but had little time for it while I was trying to attract the opposite sex.

Much to my regret, this reading curiosity stopped after a couple of years when extra-curricular activities began to play a bigger part in my life than did books. It wasn't that I was a poor reader or no longer had an interest in books, but there just didn't seem to be enough hours in the day to set aside one or two for reading. My interest became less when I read books that took four or five chapters to get interesting. Being impatient and becoming increasingly disgusted, I returned too many books to the library having read only half the book. But I didn't give up books completely and now and then and here and there, I read . . . sometimes because I wanted to and most of the time because it was required.

The love of books faded when I was near eleven. Sports of all types and Camp Fire Girl activities occupied most of my time. In junior high school, I could barely manage to read the five books assigned each semester.

Two activities, tennis and band, which were begun about the same time, the fifth grade, had a definite influence on my reading. As both of these activities called for a great deal of practice and as it was difficult for me to spell and read, I found little use or time for free reading.

It was in seventh grade that I really began to dislike reading. The only time I ever read was when I had to in literature class. I hated to write book reports, so I only read the minimum required. We had a library in our literature classroom and were free to go there after finishing other work or during free reading time. My biggest problem was that I never found any book I really liked. Eventually I just gave up and read nothing but comic books. The teacher never offered any guidance as it was his belief that "water would seek its own level."

In junior high grades became more important and the stacks of books from the public library decreased.

By the time high school began I had become totally alienated from the system of education I was familiar with. I felt it was "avant garde" to be ignorant. So I just dropped out. I read nothing but road signs and beer labels.

As my junior high days went by, there was a real need not being fulfilled in my reading I am sure, and I am not sure to just what it can be attributed. I made no attempt to read anything more than comics, magazines or any material my peers were reading, and certainly, I made no attempt to raise my level of reading interests for a few years. Part of this was due to the fact that I think I didn't want to make my gang feel I was doing any more than they were, which at the time I know made sense.

High School Years

In high school my reading was not what it should have been since we were never permitted to read outside library books in the study hall. Not staying at home for high school, I found it difficult to find a time and a place for personal reading. Weekends when I was home, I was always busy with clothing preparations and such. Then to get a book from the public library cost $3.00 a year for a card or 10 cents a book. At 10 cents a book in depression days, I was quite careful to use the minimum for book reports.

In high school I became emotionally disturbed to the point of receding into my world of books and finally in my senior year, into a state of depression. Books, school books especially, became a threat. They were something which had to be read in order to try and maintain the grade point which to me was a symbol of security. I recovered back into a world of more happiness, but I had lost most of my love of reading. Later I became convinced that fiction stories were meant for children and of no practical value to adults. I began to regret that I had not read more factual material in high school.

I remember the hours of agony which accompanied the oral book reports. I recall feeling guilty about not reading more books than I did, but I felt I wanted to live my own life rather than read about others. I gradually began to read only when a book report was due. The English teacher scolded the class because he felt the students were not reading enough, but he never guided anyone's reading selection.

Reading in high school hit an all time low. Our high school library was not very well organized. I would read books only if they were strongly recommended by others. I never liked literature in high school. *Julius Caesar* and *A Tale of Two Cities* were made to be pure misery.

However, in high school my fiction reading slowed down considerably, because I was very interested in music and my spare time was spent on this. My reading during these years was only that which was required.

Since my eighth year, piano lessons, dancing lessons and later the clarinet in the high school band occupied the greater part of my waking hours. In reality I did not have a great deal of spare time. But at the very heart of the matter, it seems to me, is the fact, unbelievable as it may seem that in spite of all of the reading which was required in the way of book reports and daily assignments for English as well as for other subjects, I had never come to the realization that literature was or could be concretely related to life. Yes, the reading which had been done had had characters, people, but they had never been real.

In high school, in the teacher's eyes, I took a turn for the worse as far as English was concerned. Sports such as basketball, football and baseball took precedence over everything else. It seemed as though boys weren't supposed to like poetry, literature, etc. . . . leave it to the girls. And I did. The only reading I did was the minimum amount required: for English (6 reports a year), History (2), Physics (2) and this was the sum total of my high school reading.

Our high school was fairly hard academically. At night I usually had from three to five hours of homework. Because of this and extra-curricular activities, I did little reading that was not required.

Reprise

Granted, some people are not interested in reading; however, the samples that have been presented in this book came from individuals who chose professions that presupposed their having an interest in books. Therefore, these people might be assumed to be reading-minded individuals. That is why it is interesting to examine their responses to learn about the experiences, if any, that turned them away from what should have been a normal activity. One should note that the preschool protocols contain no such references. Those who were read to by some caring family member remembered those experiences as happy, satisfying moments. The experiences that disrupted their reading pleasure occurred at some later date, during their public education. A few of these negative experiences even happened as late as college or thereafter.

There is little doubt that children imitate the interests of the adults around them. The child who does not see parents or siblings reading is cut off from one of the stimuli that creates a reader. One girl mentioned that her mother talked about reading and that she took after her. A boy explained that he thought only girls read and that boys took part in sports; the influence of his role models worked against his chances of becoming a reader. Another writer suggested that the lack of books at school dampened the enthusiasm for reading. The youngster who moved constantly from school to school blamed his hodgepodge instruction for his lack of interest in reading.

The most tragic of all the records, however, are those describing the traumatic experiences that children had with teachers and other adults. They were told they were poor readers, which made them feel inadequate as human beings and thereby fueled their determination to stay as far away as possible from this demeaning activity. Others became embarrassed in front of their classmates because of their teachers' comments about their poor oral reading skills. And still others were forced to read books that they found distasteful because these books were beyond either their comprehension or their interests.

Educators such as the "Bo-Peep" teacher who "leaves them alone" and the "Old Woman in the Shoe" teacher who "whips them all soundly" may equally discourage or frustrate students' enthusiasm for reading. Apparently, teachers not only must care about reading and kindling an enthusiasm for books in their students, but also have a sensitivity toward their students' needs. Ridicule of performance or denial of access to books should have no place in the reading experience. A demand for perfection should never be allowed to "club to death" the learning of any skill. As mentioned in chapter 9, instructors in the upper levels of the schools need to reconsider the merits of traditional book reports. Certainly, there is an irony in comments which indicate that making good grades in school precluded personal reading.

A few of the respondents mentioned eye problems or headaches as probable sources of their failure to enjoy reading. It comes as no surprise to find that several who grew up in the 1960s and 1970s blamed an addiction to watching television as the major reason for not reading. Others indicated a preference for activities such as music, sports, religion, and clubs for their lack of interest in or time for reading. While many respondents indicated that, at some point in their lives, they stopped reading for a while, usually because of outside activities, most did not do so for an extended period of time. But the protocols selected for this chapter were written by those who indicated that their nonreading periods went on for a long time.

This collection of responses only emphasizes the need for parents and educators to recognize that books and reading may not be the only activity in human life, but that they need to offer young people a tool for both knowledge and pleasure that provides almost unlimited value in its rewards. All adults working with the young and their reading should realize that what they, as adults, say, what they demand, and what they infer in their teaching will affect these young people over their lifetime and not always in a positive way.

14 Final Discussion

Some years ago a series of advertisements used this opening phrase: "Give me a man who reads." The implication was that, in any field, whether electronics or auto mechanics, nursing or counseling, housewifery or rocketry, the person who reads has the most important qualifications for growth on the job. This is, of course, only one advertiser's opinion, but it poses a valid question. Just how important is reading? Certainly, the ability to read is a skill considered the birthright of every American and the foundation for our democracy. The success of an educational system is often judged by the literacy rate of its products. Great sums are expended annually across the country to identify those relatively few young people who, for one reason or another, have failed to profit from the usual reading instruction in the early school years. At least we seem to give lip service to the importance of each citizen's knowing how to read. "Every person a reader" might well be our slogan.

But how do we promote this skill? What really happens to young people's reading of books as they move up through our educational system? Are their experiences with books alike or different? Does a reader's maturation consist of broad leaps or small steps? This picture is the one that we have tried to encapsulate through the voices of many individuals who wrote about their lives with books.

Theorists have long pointed out distinctions in different kinds of reading: one of the most common is between informational and recreational reading. In general, American society is more interested in the first type of reading than in the second. Elementary reading programs have moved steadily away from recreational reading toward informational reading. Actually, however, the two are closely related. As expressive writing is the parent of expository writing, so recreational reading is the parent from which informational reading springs. If one is asked to describe "the person who reads," one pictures an individual reading for recreational purposes. We see that person as reading novels, biographies, histories, or idea-oriented materials rather than books about how to use a computer or how to repair a car. We see these people on planes, at the doctor's office, in an armchair after dinner,

145

or in bed before falling asleep. They are not out to advance themselves but to fulfill themselves: "Reading maketh a full man."

The people who wrote these autobiographies over a period of nearly thirty years subscribe to a similar definition of the "reading man (or woman)." They were asked simply to describe their experiences in growing up with books and reading. Although they were not asked to limit their discussions to experiences with recreational reading, nonetheless their experiences with recreational reading dominate their autobiographies. Would the writers have interpreted the assignment differently if they had been budding engineers, physicians, or lawyers? We think not.

Conditions That Promote Reading

Availability of Books and Magazines

If individuals are surrounded with books, magazines, and newspapers, they will read. Books need to be in the home, whether in the attic or bathroom, on bookshelves or in boxes. Ideally, reading material should be everywhere possible: in locker rooms and schoolrooms, in churches and recreational buildings, on buses and planes, in barber shops and beauty shops, in waiting rooms and theaters. One library authority (district) in England placed paperbacks in youth clubs and at playing fields and found there were many takers. The records show that once people learn to read, they become excited at finding books in unexpected places. Some readers even delight in reading the inside of matchbook covers, bus transfers, and cereal boxes.

Family Members Who Read Aloud

Obviously, the initial stage of enjoyment is through the ear. When parents, siblings, grandparents, aunts, and uncles read stories aloud, reminisced, recited poetry, and told tall tales, the young were always fascinated. But listening is important not only in the prereading stage. The writers of the protocols tell of their joy during elementary school when a teacher read books aloud. Sometimes they were afraid that school would end before the final chapter had been reached. Teenagers' appreciation of the classics seems to develop from the oral renditions by talented teachers. Even in college classrooms, students recall the pleasure of having a professor read passages aloud from the books under discussion. Oral reading is so successful a technique with most age groups that it can be called one of the "never-fail methods" for the teaching of literature. Today, books in cassette form are proving a popular way for the public to hear literature as they drive, walk, or jog.

Adults and Peers Who Read

The majority of the respondents came from reading homes although there were a few who said, quite frankly, that their families were nonreaders. Not everyone came from a middle-class home, and for some writers, only a few books were present, the purchase of each one having been considered carefully. In many households, family members not only read for their own enjoyment, but also read aloud to the children from material such as a medical journal or a new novel. Older siblings read and brought home books from the library or their college classes. Homes had books lying about, and some of the most memorable reading seemed to be done in bathrooms. Children admired those who could recite poetry, and they sometimes learned to recite some of the verses themselves. One respondent learned the stories from Gilbert and Sullivan operettas and could sing the songs from *The Mikado* because her mother enjoyed singing them as well.

Role Models Who Value Reading

One might assume that if the parents read, they, themselves, valued reading. But valuing reading goes a step beyond mere performance. Placing value on reading implies that one makes time for reading among the multitude of other daily activities. A set time for reading and discussing books and magazines was reported as a family activity by some of the writers. Others remarked that someone took them regularly to the library and that they were issued their own library card. A number treasured a hardbound book as something special, a "real" book. Still others mentioned older siblings who either recommended books or chided their younger brothers and sisters for not improving the quality of their reading fare. In high school, discussions of books among peers challenged some of the respondents to read more in order to gain status within the group. A teacher's enthusiasm for a literary work or an author could often spark students' interest.

Sharing and Discussing Books

Reading is usually considered a solitary occupation, but it also can lead to expressive activities. Books, whether fiction or nonfiction, produce intellectual constructs in the mind of the reader. Intellectual activities, however, can be better understood and appreciated if they are externalized by talking with others. In fact, most of our use of language is for savoring and understanding our innermost thoughts. Again and again, our respondents tell of their need to talk about their reading. As children, they seemed less able to express their reactions, worrying as one did, for example, about Peter Rabbit's predicament, and yet not being able to verbalize this concern. Others felt that the boys and girls in the primers were behaving quite stupidly, but they could not discuss these feelings with others. There was one child who was so taken with the story of *Heidi* that she insisted her parents get some goat's milk so she could decide if it really did have a spicy taste; in this way, she was externalizing some of her reactions as did the girl who, being so upset by the cruelty of the people toward horses in *Black Beauty*, talked about her feelings with her parents. As adolescents, the writers talked of discussing books with their friends. Some reported that they needed to be able to express their reactions without being told what to think or how to interpret the literature they read in class. Therefore, it is not surprising to learn that, as adults, many of them joined book discussion clubs or took night school courses where they could discuss literature with others.

Owning Books

That which is precious and valuable is that which we want to own. This sentiment is reflected in the autobiographies, where the writers tell of their pride in owning books, particularly during childhood. Books were so important that the writers kept the same volumes into adult life. Christmas and birthdays are mentioned as important gift days. One individual who was enthralled by electricity and found the library selections to be inadequate, mentions that, for the first time, he asked for books at Christmas. Birthdays and periods of illness were also times at which the respondents received gift books. Some parents took their children to stores and permitted them to purchase books of their own. This was exciting for the children, even if the book was only a five- or ten-cent paperback. During the adolescent years, book clubs proved exciting for the writers by providing both choice and ownership of books. The national book clubs, with their monthly selections, became sources of books for some of these same writers when they became adults.

Availability of Libraries and Librarians

The respondents tell of the impact of the library and the librarian on their reading. They mention the excitement of securing their own library cards and using the library as a quiet, secure refuge. They also mention the librarians, usually women, who delighted them during story hours or who could lead them to exactly the type of books they wanted. Emerging from the autobiographies are some images of librarians as "guardians" of the books, whose regulations on the numbers of books that could be checked out sometimes proved frustrating. Some of the writers indicate that both the atmosphere and design of a library were important to them. But most reported only good experiences with librarians and libraries and emphasized the impact of the right kind of library on the developing reader.

Social Interaction

Many of these autobiographies indicate that reading is a social as well as a solitary phenomenon. Since budding readers often live with other readers, reading material can become a part of human interaction: not just an interaction between author and reader but between the readers, themselves. The respondents tell of reading cozily in a friend's home during the afternoons and of discussing teen romances during junior high lunch periods. They speak of the part reading played in a love affair. The book clubs for adults were not just for discussing books but for socializing with others. People have long felt that the literary heritage is an important component of a person's education, perhaps because reading a body of literature in common brings about a certain social cohesiveness. In England, some observers have remarked that social class is based not so much on wealth or birthright as it is on shared cultural experiences, one of which is a body of common reading.

Freedom of Choice in Reading Material

Sometimes the writers indicated surprising choices in their childhood reading fare, from *True Story* magazine to novels such as *Brave New World*. However, most still reported their favorites to be the familiar children's classics, nursery rhymes, and fairy tales. Particularly during the teenage years, young people want to range widely in the world of books. Those who had access to old boxes of series books indulged themselves to the point of satiation and then moved on to other types of books. Some readers seemed to revel in the approach whereby a teacher put books out on a table in smorgasbord fashion so that students could discover many types of literature and find out on their own what they most enjoyed. A few of the respondents experienced individualized reading classes during the 1960s and 1970s; they felt they were enthusiastic about reading because they were encouraged to read what they liked and because blocks of time were set aside for them to do so. These same writers tell of changes that occurred within their lives because they were exposed to a wide variety of books. Disappointingly, this type of program, which had such excellent results in creating readers, has been abandoned because it is considered an educational "frill."

Personal Experience

Books have served a variety of purposes for the respondents. For some, books have given pleasure during times of illness. (Protocols from the 1970s and 1980s mention this less frequently, probably because of television's entertainment value.) At times, books provided surrogates for human interaction. Sometimes, they were an escape from the real world or else a cautious route into it. For some readers, a book expressed, in words, what they thought were peculiarly individual experiences not shared or felt by others. (For male readers, very often *Catcher in the Rye* articulated their experiences.) For some, there were "watershed" books, which changed the direction of the reader's life, such as the boy who read *Death Be Not Proud* and then became obsessed with death. Another person so admired Eliot and his *Waste Land* that he set himself the goal of raising his level of language awareness.

School Programs

People's reading interests follow a step-by-step developmental pattern that is relatively consistent from individual to individual. These steps have been well documented in a number of scholarly studies. The protocols in this book show a typical progression in reading interests. Although the writers of the autobiographies ultimately selected professions for themselves where books were valued, the writers were not "childhood wonders" who read adult classics while in second grade. They tasted and read the usual fare of children's classics and then moved through the series books to the books on subjects that had predictable appeal for youngsters in the late elementary and early junior high school grades: subjects that included animals, adventure, and stories set during pioneer times.

As these same readers grew older, they chose to read books about teenagers who were experiencing the same physical and psychological changes in adolescence that they were. Like their peers who did not become English teachers and librarians, the writers also turned to their books for answers to troubling problems and explored the possibilities that life might offer. The book titles dealing with teenage problems have changed across the span of the autobiographies, but the same types of books, in substance, continue to be mentioned. For example, Anne Emery's books were mentioned in the autobiographies from the 1950s and Judy Blume's in those from the 1970s.

As the respondents progressed through high school, their interests broadened from concerns for self to concerns for the more complex questions that have confronted us since the beginning of time. Later on — usually during the senior year in high school or some time in college — the writers begin to mention an appreciation of literary artistry in the adult classics. Throughout most of the school experience, the readers' choices are guided by the content rather than the literary sophistication of the books they read. The chart presented in this chapter encapsulates the factors that influenced the respondents to become readers and indicates the periods of life at which their reading behavior seemed to occur. Although most of the writers of the protocols did become readers, they frequently mentioned obstacles they encountered along the way. If there are conditions that promote reading, there are also, of course, conditions that operate against it.

Conditions That Discourage Reading

Growing Up with Nonreaders

Some of the respondents grew up in nonreading families; for them, books and reading were not among their earliest recollections. These young people did not have role models in the family who read. Obviously, such families neither read aloud nor provided reading material. Moreover, the children of these families were not taken to libraries or stores in order to find books to read. Ultimately, these people had to depend on teachers and librarians for recommendations about books and reinforcement for reading.

Traumatic Learning Experiences

Evidently, many of the respondents found that reading ahead was a gross infringement of the rules when they were in a reading group. It would seem that some teachers cannot accommodate the special child. Some writers of the autobiographies were traumatized by having to read in front of a group. Others were embarrassed by their mispronouncing words. Still others were threatened and sometimes actually hit with a ruler when a word was mispronounced. And there

Experiences Likely to Produce Readers

	Age groups (in years)					
	2–5	6–8	9–11	12–14	15–17	18+
Hearing rhythm and sounds of words	X	X				
Seeing adults read	X	X	X			
Finding books around the house	X	X	X			
Pretending to read	X					
Voluntarily memorizing favorite stories	X	X				
Participating in reading stories and rhymes	X	X				
Being read to by family members	X	X				
Receiving praise for developing reading skills		X				
Acting out stories	X	X	X			
Developing reading skills at their own pace		X				
Visiting the library with a loved one	X	X	X			
Rereading favorite stories		X	X			
Setting aside time for reading		X	X	X	X	
Having a teacher show interest in the individual's reading		X	X	X	X	
Having teachers read aloud		X	X	X	X	X

	Age groups (in years)					
	2–5	6–8	9–11	12–14	15–17	18+
Being exposed to a variety of reading fare		X	X	X		
Becoming fascinated with one subject		X				
Receiving help from librarians		X	X	X		
Owning books			X	X	X	X
Finding a system for reading			X			
Participating in reading contests			X			
Sharing books with friends			X	X	X	X
Participating in reader-centered discussions of literature		X	X	X	X	
Generating nontraditional book reports			X	X	X	
Being allowed freedom of choice in reading fare		X	X	X	X	X

were those who had a negative self-image and thought of themselves as "poor" readers; since they could not read well, they avoided reading situations in their early years.

Sometimes experiences with libraries and librarians discouraged young readers. They resented the rules about the number of books they could check out as well as the age restrictions for use of the adult collection. For some, librarians seemed like ogres who inhabited dark and forbidding realms. The atmosphere of the library was carried over to the books that were housed there; a forbidding ambience made reading seem a forbidden activity.

Obstacles during the Teenage Years

The teenage years bring about different impediments to reading. One of these is the time required by other activities: sports, music, clubs, expanding social life, school assignments, church activities, and dating. If reading is to be kept alive, it seems imperative that time for free reading should be set aside as part of the school day. Some respondents complained that adult classics were introduced too early in the classroom. Parents and educators have long been paranoid about the age at which a child should learn to read, so the first grade has become sacrosanct as the right time, a questionable assumption in scientific findings. The same inflexibility is shown when the classics are assigned to students: the sooner, the better is the watchword. Yet this early exposure is refuted in the protocols. Some writers revealed that they were absolutely baffled by the classics, which are assigned, today, as early as the sixth grade. Others professed shame that they found them dull as teenagers and really liked mysteries and adventure stories better. Some respondents withdrew completely from the world of books because the classics were so far beyond their level of reading ability.

Educational Methodology

Book reports were almost universally disliked by the respondents. Book reports did more to kill the young people's interest in reading than to promote it. Some writers were traumatized by oral presentations, even when the presentations were about books they actually enjoyed reading. Granted, required book reports are a legitimate effort on the part of teachers to foster reading and to make some attempt to broaden the reading tastes of their students; a few of the protocols indicate that the reports did accomplish these aims. But for most of the respondents, book reports became a source of irritation, ranging from mild to violent dislike on the part of the writers. The protocols showed young people resorting to all kinds of subterfuges when faced with doing the mandatory book report.

Another activity that was frequently despised by the writers was the "literary notebook." The literary notebook contained collections of pictures or original sketches, quotations, some attempts at creative writing, and always an elaborate cover. What once started out as a method for broadening students' awareness of literature or of a particular selection has generally produced the opposite effect.

The intensive study of a single work by a class over a long period of time — as much as six weeks or longer — also tended to decrease student interest in the selection. Frequently the autobiographies indicated that the respondents finished reading the work within a day or two after it was assigned and then spent weeks of boredom as the class members slowly inched their way through it together. Consequently, their enthusiasm for the work and the author was sadly diminished.

In the secondary schools, students were impatient and baffled by the search for "the meaning" in a literary work. Their own "response" to the piece of writing was never enough. While interpretation of a literary work must mean a balance between a response and substantiation in the text of the work, many teachers led their students to believe that there was a "correct meaning" and that the teacher's meaning was the only possible one. If students failed to agree, they became mystified with literature, and it became an incomprehensible world which they could not enter. Frustrated, some simply quit reading.

Here then are the conclusions that we have drawn from the more than one thousand reading autobiographies collected over nearly thirty years. The autobiographies preserve a record of how people remember their experiences with reading and books from their earliest years up through maturity. At times, the process may have a strange forward and backward movement. There are surprising accidents that make people readers; for others, there are just as many occurrences that keep them from becoming so. Efforts in the classroom that are designed to make young people readers were sometimes profitable and at other times detrimental. Perhaps the old farmer's comment, "I know how to farm twice as good as I do" might be applied to our teaching of reading: we know how to make readers out of people "twice as good as we do." The voices are clear and strong in articulating the direction that reading instruction should follow. The advertiser's injunction "Give me a person who reads" is but a modern echo of Bacon's statement, "Reading maketh a full man."

Authors

G. Robert Carlsen holds a Ph.D. in English education from the University of Minnesota and is professor emeritus in English and education from the University of Iowa. He has authored over seventy professional articles as well as *Books and the Teenage Reader* and has coauthored (with James Brown) the *Brown-Carlsen Test of Listening Comprehension*. He was general editor of *Themes and Writers*. Professor Carlsen is a former President of NCTE and has received distinguished service awards from NCTE, (the first ever offered by) the Assembly on Literature for Adolescents of NCTE (ALAN), the Secondary Section of NCTE, and the Iowa Council of Teachers of English, among others.

Anne Sherrill holds a Ph.D. in English education from the University of Iowa and is associate professor of English at East Tennessee State University, where she teaches courses in literature for adolescents and in children's literature. She has delivered and published numerous professional papers and is the coauthor (with Paula Robertson-Rose) of *Four Elements: A Creative Approach to the Short Story.*